Bono, Lizzy and the Rats

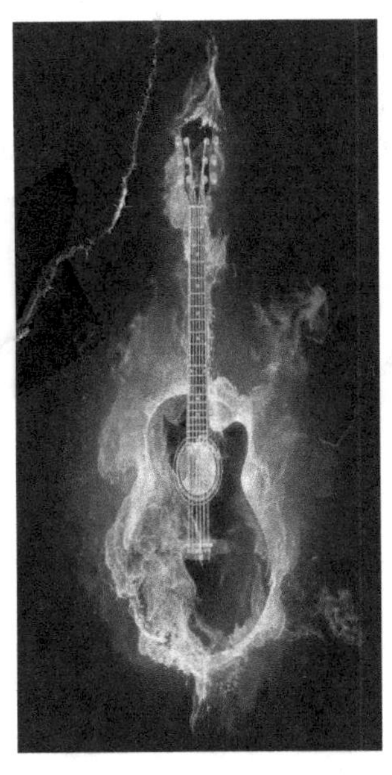

Ex Libris

Publisher.
Dun Emer Press.
2nd Flr, 13 Upr Baggot St, Dublin 4.
Registered in the Writers Guild LA.
Contact ; G Murray . pegasusagent123@gmail.com

Bono, Lizzy and the Rats

The story of Irish rock

the music that changed

the world.

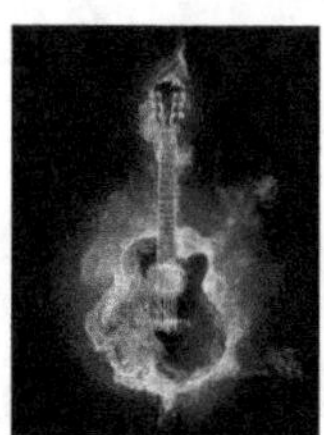

Gabriel Murray

Dun Emer Press

Introduction;

A novel based on the early days of Irish rock when Phil Lynott (Thin Lizzy) Bono (U2) and Bob Geldof (The Boom Town Rats) blazed a trail across Dublin. The days when U2 played for fifty pence, at the Dandelion Flea Market, Bob Geldof worked in an abattoir and Phil Lynott busked on Grafton street. All became world famous rock stars. This is the story of their humble beginnings in the clubs of Dublin.

Thin Lizzy;

Founded in Dublin in 1969 by Phil Lynott and his school friend Brian Downey, Thin Lizzy was named after the nickname for the Ford Model T (The Tin Lizzy). With Lynott as lead singer, they went on to record 13 hard rock albums. It's hard to listen to any classic rock radio station in the USA or Europe and not hear one or two Thin Lizzy songs. With hits like The Boys Are Back in Town, waiting for an Alibi, Jailbreak, Whiskey In The Jar, Thin Lizzy were a big hit amongst Irish people. The band had many rocky times over the years, with drug addiction and infighting causing problems amongst band members. Phil Lynott sadly died in 1986. In the late 1970s, Thin Lizzy were often referred to as the greatest hard rock band on the planet.

The Boomtown Rats.

This punk rock band hail from Dun Laoghaire, Co. Dublin, but moved to London in 1976 to join that city's vibrant punk rock scene. Led by Bob Geldof, the band produced many memorable hits in the 80's like Banana Republic, I Don't Like Mondays, Like Clockwork, and Rat Trap. Bob Geldof was the driving force behind the Band Aid Supergroup in 1984, and Live Aid concerts in 1985. The Boomtown Rats were the first Irish band to make number 1 in the UK charts with the song Rat Trap, and again repeated the following year with I Don't Like Mondays.

U 2.

Formed in 1976 after Larry Mullen posted an ad on a school notice board looking for musicians, this Dublin band has taken the world by storm and really put Ireland on the musical map. U2 have sold over 150 million records making them one of the bestselling bands of all time.

Remembering Philo. Hot press Article excerpt;11 March 2011.

'He was an amazing front man. If that lyrical, musical ability has to be matched with showmanship, attitude, style, if that's your version of rock 'n' roll – there's no way past Phil Lynott. He's at the top of the tree." Bono.

This book is dedicated to;

Bill Graham, (1951 – 1996)

Shay Healy (1943 – 2021)

Thom Mc Ginty (1952 – 1995)

Philomena Lynott (1930-2019)

David Edward Sutch (1940 – 1999)

Do you not get it, lads? The Irish are the blacks of

Europe. And Dubliners are the blacks of Ireland. And the Northside Dubliners are the blacks of Dublin. So say it once, say it loud: I'm black and I'm proud.

Roddy Doyle –The Commitments.

Elizabeth's letter to the author; Jan 5 – 2013.

Sometimes think of him. The way he was. How he blazed a trail across Dublin, in the early seventies and then for sixteen years across the world. I knew him and I loved him. He loved me too. Phil was one of a kind. He was like all great heroes. They come and shine a light into our world and like a candle in the wind they burn out. Philips flame lasted thirty-six years. He like many great stars, Janis Joplin, Jim Morrison and Jimi Hendrix, burned out long before they lived out their natural days. Philip helped so many people, like U2 and The Boom Town Rats, launch their careers. They belonged to a music, that I believed changed the world. If you want to recreate the story. Please read all my love letters to Phil and return them to me safely. It is the untold story of Irish rock. My name is Elizabeth. Some people used to call me Thin Lizzy.

My best wishes to you, Lizzy.

Lizzy and the Rats

Dublin 1968 - 1976.

A golden sunset hung beyond Crumlin's canal. Phil Lynott lines up and collects his welfare money.

He carries his guitar, that is covered in stickers, of the Stones, the Beatles and the Who.

***

Phil makes his way to Molloy's pub. He meets his uncle Pete, in the back room, with his band the Black Eagles.

-Jasus Philo, your late, were on in five minutes. Have you learnt that guitar yet?

-Not yet!

-Look, you can sing, so come on stage and give it a blast.

-Ok, uncle Pete, whatever you say.

Phil nervously walks on stage and is handed a mike by Pete.

Phil's and Pete belt out 'I remember that summer in Dublin'. The pub is packed and full of smoke. Pete nods to Phil. The crowd joins in the singing.

I remember that summer in Dublin,

And the Liffey as it stank like hell,

And young people walking down Grafton Street, everyone looking so well.

I was singing a song I heard somewhere, called "Rock'n'Roll Never Forget",

***

At the end of the evening, they all go back to Pete's

House, to listen to some music. Pete puts on a record of a band called the Stax.

-That's what I call music, real music, soul the black man's music. You're one of them Phil, that's what you've got to listen to, its your roots Phil! If you want to be a rock star. I've got a surprise for you. Peter takes out an electric guitar from its case.

-You can burn the 'bollocks' out of this one. It's a real beauty, It's electric. It's called a Stratocaster.

-A stratocaster?

-A Stratocaster Phil - got it?

-You've got to learn the jargon if you want to get into the game.

Peter plugged it in to the mains and started playing. The sound was unbelievable, blaring out through the whole house.

-It's fantastic! Said Phil.

-Here, you have a try. I'm popping out to get some whisky. Peter handed Phil the guitar and walked out.

Phil's Gran walked in, her face black like thunder.

-Phil, I told you, Peter not to bring that thing into the

house. Can't you play a normal instrument? Something like a guitar?

-It is a guitar, an electric guitar.

-In my day there was ballroom dancing Why don't you take Claire down for a dance? She'd love that, she would.

-I'll pay for your tickets. Put on a nice suit and comb that mop of hair of yours. It looks like something you'd wax the floor with!

-That's an afro, Gran.

-Afrogran, what's that?

-You know, afro from the Caribbean, like I'm black, remember?

-You're black all right, but I remember your father with

A good short back and sides, a real regulation haircut, like a real man.

-But I want it to grow it longer.

-You'll turn into one of those weirdos on the beat scene.

Peter returns, with a bottle of whisky.

-Leave him alone, will you? He's just growing up. - Not like the rest of the boys round here! How are you going to get a decent job, looking like that?

-Gran, I don't want a decent job - working in a factory, or in a chipper.

-You'll take what you can get. Beggars can't be choosers. What about college?

-I don't want a nine to five job.

-You're a bad influence on the boy, Peter. That music is only for a crowd of hair brained loonies. ***

Later Phil turns on the television and watches 'High Noon'. Gary Cooper aims at the villain and shoot's him dead. Phil's eyes are glued to the screen. Looking in the mirror, he adopts the film star's pose. He opens his wardrobe and takes out a cowboy hat, tie and boots. He tries them on and looks in the mirror, combing his hair and slapping on some afters have.

Peter taps on the door and enters.

-That's real cool, Phil, you look like a right eejit!

Where did ya get the gear, in the bleeding wax museum?

-Piss off! Replied Phil. Arranging the tie, which looks like a shoe lace.

-What's that, Phil?

-A tie.

Peter laughs out loud.

-It looks like a shoelace to me. Are ye's going down to the local ballroom?

-It was gran's idea, not mine. She's paying for it!

***

Gran got her way. She bought Phil two tickets for the

Crumlin road ballroom. He put on his best gear. He arranged to meet Claire. Two skinheads with, Alsatian dogs started heckling him from, the other side of the road.

-Hey ya, 'black bastard!

Phil stopped and stared, a murderous look in his eyes. The dog snarled. Phil decided to walk on. He reached the ballroom where Claire stood waiting outside. She looked cute in a red dress. The queue of people shuffled excitedly under the signpost, which read Dickie Rock.

The queue started moving. Claire and Phil walk in, arm in arm.

The band starts to play. Dickie Rock begins to sing. Phil grabs hold of Claire and sweeps her onto the dance floor. A skinhead strolls up to them, staring menacingly.

The Dickie Rock singer on stage swings, his hips.

The skinhead, poker faced, stares at Phil.

-Hey, 'nigger', why don't you get back to the jungle?

-Are you talk'in to me? You look like you need a broken nose, you fat-arsed slob.

Phil stares at him intensely. The skinhead throws a

punch. Phil's hand goes up to block it. Then gives him a head butt. The skinhead screams in pain and collapses to the floor. One of his friends joins in and a fight erupts; chairs and tables fly through the air.

-You're not wanted round here, 'nigger' boy.

-Phil, don't ... Dont! screams Claire.

The skinhead lunges forward, supported by his friends. Other boys back Phil. A fight breaks out. They punch each other. Police sirens sing through the air. Everybody disperses. Phil tries to take on the skinhead, but he is no match for him; the thug kicks him mercilessly and he falls to the ground. Helpless, he lays there being kicked. Blood runs from his nose.

Outside, an ambulance arrives and shrieks to a halt. Ambulance men come in and lift Phil onto a stretcher. He is carried away.

***

In the hospital corridor, a doctor stands talking to Phil's gran and Uncle Pete.

-I'm afraid it's hard to say how, he is still in intensive care.

-Please let me go and see him, begs Phil's Gran.

The doctor leads the way. Inside the intensive care unit. Phil lays on a drip. His Gran hurries in, tears in her eyes. Phils gran, bends over Phil's face and kisses his cheek.

-You're gonna be alright, Phil, she whispers.

Peter comes up behind her and put his hands on her shoulder. Phil nurses his right eye.

-I'll get those bastards, that fatso is a real gurrier! Said Pete. I know his father, a docker from the northside. You should never trust a north-sider. You're black and you're Irish, be proud of it, Phil. I'll tell ya, it was different in my day, they had some respect.

Later that night Claire visits him.

-Phil are you ok!

-I'll survive!

-You look sad and depressed Phil.

-I was thinking about my father, the father I never had. Lying here brings back memories. Phil said, softly. Gran always used to talk about him. He knew how to dance the tango.

-But you never had one!

-Everybody's got an old man somewhere. I've heard he was a cowboy.

-Well you're a bit of a cowboy yourself, aren't you Phil?

-Where is is he now? The auld bollox!

-I wish I knew. He was a South American sailor, you know. Maybe a cowboy too.

-You're a right bleedin sailor, Philo.

***

Inside Dino's Bar, in Crumlin village, Phil meets his old school friend, Brian Downey.

-Hi Brian, how's it going?

-What have you been up to?

-Playing drums with Sugar Shack, but it's going nowhere.

-Fine Phil, how are you?

-I want to get out of Crumlin. I love and hate the place, when you're on the rock and roll, it's a pain in the arse around here. cracking the scene in Dublin here is not easy. replied Phil.

-Well if I can't do it Philo, nobody else can.

-I'm putting a band together. Said Brian.

-Have you a name for the band yet? Replied Phil.

-Yeah, The Orphanage!

-I feel like an orphan!

-Drop around I've got a garage at the back of my house for a practice session. I have too new band members; Pat Quigley on bass and Joe Staunton on guitar.

***

Phil walks down the road with Brian. He drops in for some cigarettes at a corner shop.

-Twenty Major. Said Phil.

The shopkeeper takes the money and hands him the cigarettes. He looks at Phil.

-Don't tell me, I know where you're from, Jamaica.

Phil looks at Brian amused Brian smiles back at aim. - I'm from Crumlin, I'm Irish!

-Well, you're the first black Irishman, I have ever seen around here!

-Well you'll be seeing a lot more of us around here! Phil exits, slamming the door. It is raining heavily outside.

-Where are you off to?

-Up Grafton street to busk.

-It's bloody raining!

-Well, I'm broke! I need a few quid. Anyway, I've got a good spot outside Captain America's.

-Yeah, it's Ireland's first hamburger joint! Said Phil.

***

Phil spots a young gypsy boy, driving a horse and carriage which carries some old bathtubs. He calls out to the boy.

-Paddy, are you heading up Grafton Street?

The gypsy boy came to a halt.

-Get on, Philo. He muttered.

-See ya later.

Phil waived to Brian and watched him disappear along the canal road.

***

Phil strolls down Grafton Street with his guitar when Macker, a well-known drug-dealer, approached him.

-Want any hash Phil? he asked.

-Macker, I'm broke!

-I'm looking for the price of a hamburger myself.

-Get into dealing, Phil. It's the only way to make any bread around here.

-Well, if rock and roll doesn't work, I'll think about it.

Phil replied.

***

Phil walked down South Anne's street, to the burger bar - Captain America's and stands beneath the neon sign. He took his guitar and started playing the Hendrix number, 'If six were nine'.

'White-collar conservatives flashing down the street

They're hoping soon my kind will drop and die,

A black man wearing an American soldier's cap approaches Phil, with a big smile.

-How's it goin' brother? Where are you from?

-Dublin, Phil replied.

-Well, I'll be darned, a black Irishman. You're another brother like me. Us brothers should stick together; we're out-numbered round here.

-Where are you from? asked Phil, curiously.

-Harlem, New York. Do you know any soul songs?

-The names Joe, GI Joe!

-Yeah! How about you?

-Phil, Phil Lynott.

-Well Phil, listen to this and put some music to it, he said, in a confident tone.

GI Joe starts singing a gospel song. Phil joins in, playing his guitar. A crowd gathered around them and stood listening under their umbrellas in the rain. GI Joe puts his hat on the pavement. Little by little the crowd drops coins into it.

***

Phil and the GI Joe, goes inside the burger bar, to spend the takings. They sit down together and ordered a burger.

-Look, man, I'm into soul, I'm into rock, anything that'll make that guitar sing, you know what I mean, man?

Show me that thing. G.I. Joe takes the guitar in his hands.

-Now, remember man, the guitar is like a woman, you've

got to make love to it, you've got to hold it like a woman, caress it like a woman, pluck it, hold it. But remember man, that sound has to come from deep inside and you got to bring it out. It's all about foreplay, you bring the audience up where they belong, do you get it, brother?

GI Joe lets the guitar strings rip, singing in a deep melodious tone and rhythmically swaying his body. The diners applaud.

***

The went outside. Joe rolls a joint and hands it to Phil.

-This is real one hundred per cent Moroccan, try it Phil.

Phil noticed a scar on Joe's arm.

-Where did you get that?

-Nam, Phil in Nam.

-Vietnam, you mean!

-That's right, man. Two years in that place, and believe me, once you do time in Nam. You just think of getting out alive. That's why they called me the cat, the black cat with nine lives. I've lived more lives than a cat.

-So how did you get to Dublin?

-I took the banana boat from Jamaica. I want to forget. Do you know what it's like to look down the end of a loaded barrel?

Joe lifted his headband and showed Phil a gash in his head.

Jasus, Joe, where did you get that?

-Rats Phil, it's a specialist Vietcong torture. They tie this cage to your head, with a hungry rat inside, a very hungry rat, Phil. A rat that hasn't seen a square meal in weeks. Man when that rat sees its square meal, all that curly hair, wrapped around your brain man, its gets hungry. Those Vietcong, are bad bastards.

-How did you get out of there?

-Well, I gave that bastard, such a kick in the balls. I dropped him man, then I gave him the Harlem head butt. Then I took his knife and slit his throat. ***

On his way home from Grafton St, Phil drops into Mc Gonagles, to meet with Brush Shields and his band Skid Row. Brush sports long hair appearing beneath a berry cap. Phil meets him, at the bar.

-Have a pint, Phil.

-How's Skid Row getting on?

-Great Phil, no bother.

-Yes,

-I still need some lessons!

-I have a new guitar.

Brush shows him a Fender Jazz guitar.

-Jesus, Brush, it's a beauty.

-Can you teach me how to play?

-Sure but I'll teach you four strings not six.

-Whats, up Brush. You wanted to talk to me.
- Why don't you join Skid Row and be a front
man. You look good Phil, that's what the
women want. When you're up to speed, you
can play the guitar.

-Cool, Brush. you're a real friend.

-Meet the band. This is Noel Bridgeman on
drums and Bernie Cheevers on lead guitar.

-Can you sing Phil. Give us a blast. Said
Noel.

-Ok. Said Phil getting up on stage. Only a few
people have arrived so Phil dident feel too
nervous.

-How about 'You got me Floatin' By Jim
Hendrix.

You got me floatin' round and round,

Always up, you never let me down…

Jasus Phil, you have a voice, cool stuff. Said Brian.

So are you in.

-I'm in. But boys, I want to set up my own band with my own sound and lyrics someday.

Cool, Phil. We understand. Said Brush clapping him on his back.

***

Phil drops in to meet Brian in a back street garage in

Crumlin. He meets new band members of 'The Orphanage', Joe and Pat, Robbie, Scott.

-Great to meet you Pat, Joe.

-Love the afro Phil, it's cool. Said Joe.

-Yeah, cool said Pat slinging his guitar strap around his neck.

-So Phil, Brian tells us you're with Skid Row.

-Yeah, but Brush is into his own thing. I am not sure I will last their long. I want my own band.

-Give us a blast of something. What songs do you know? How about a Beatles song?

-Don't know that one. How about –The Beatle's 'Hey Jude'

-Cool. Said Brian hitting the drums.

Phil starts to sing. The boys are impressed.

-Hey Jude don't make it bad.

Take a sad song and make it better,

-Nice sound Phil, You're a natural. Said Brian.

***

A week later Phil went with to sing at gig in a pub in Rathmines with Skid Row. He gave it all he had full blast until he though his voice would crack.

Only five people showed up. They forgot it was football night so they lads were at home watching the game. They drowned their sorrows at the bar with a few free pints from the pub owner. ***

Later on in the evening is Phil at home, in his bedroom. He has his head stuck in a bucket of water. He was just coming up to grasp for breath, when his Gran walks in.

-What in heaven are you doing Philip?

Phil spoke to her a quiet voice, his face streaming with water.

-Jesus granma, Brush was teaching me how to hold my breath

-What for?

-Oh, for the singing!

-What singing?

For the, rock band I'm going to set up.

-A rock band, what will you be up to next, what about a good job?

-I don't know Gran, If I want one!

***

Phil had pushed his vocal cords too far; He lay in bed. He could not speak. Phil looked on deaths door. Pete called the doctor. A few hours later, he was in hospital having his tonsils out. Phil woke up to find Pete and Gran staring at him.

31

-You blew your tonsils Phil. You have to take it easy. Said Pete.

-Yes, Phil, rest up. Said Gran caressing his forehead.

Phil was laid up for weeks.

***

He was just out of bed a few days when he ran into Brush in Dino's bar. He told him that he had a new singer for the band. He was worried that he would not only blow his tonsils, but his vocal cords. ***

Phil called around to Brian's garage. He could hear the drums down the alleyway. A few minutes later, Brian agreed to make him the lead singer of the Orphanage.

***

One evening Phil ventured into Phil into the Baggot Inn. He stood sipping his pint at the bar when, someone approached him. He held out his hand.

-How do you do, my name's Smiley Bolger.
- How's it going Smiley?

-Look man, I'm a D.J, Journalist, Radio Promoter.

-Sounds good. I need an agent. I want a few gigs.

-It's controlled by the show band circuit. I'm your man. I'll get you a gig.

-Well Smiley, maybe you'll get me my first break, into rock stardom. Have a pint.

-I'm yer man Philo, yes I'm yer man, answered Smiley with a wide grin.

***

A few days later Smiley managed to arrange a meeting between Phil and a music agent. Phil walked boldly into the office. The walls were lined with pictures of show bands. The agent, who was balding and overweight and sat there smoking a cigar.

-You're wasting your time here, Phil. Said the agent.

The Irish aren't interested in rock and roll. They want the big show bands like Brendan Bower swinging his hips like Elvis doing the 'Huckle Buck'. England's the place for you.

-What the name of your band?

-The Orphanage.

-Sound crap!

-Can't you give us a break? Just line us up on a tour of the ballrooms! Pleaded Phil.

-It just won't work. The show bands have it all sewn up. You're just hanging round here in Ireland. Why don't

you just be like other paddies and get the boat, to England?

A young man walks in with a contract and places it on the desk.

-This is Louis Walsh, he launching a singer called Johnny Logan. This is Phil Lynott he has a band called The Orphanage. Hes looking for a few gigs.

-I have a ballroom in Kiltimagh that may be able to help you.

-Where that. Said Phil.

-Co Mayo.

-Sorry I need a Dublin gig.

-I am busy right now with Johnny; he's going to win the Eurovision. I am sure of it.

-What's that?

-It's a big TV show for singers across Europe. It's not for you Phil. You're a rocker, the real deal. Look if I hear of anything I'll call you. This is my card.

-Thanks' Louis.

-People love rock, but they love the crooners. Frank Sinatra, Bing Crosby if you can find a good looking boy singing that kind of stuff you will make millions. Rock and roll has its place but boy bands is the future. Phil wasn't going to give up that easily. He struck up a friendship with the agent and his friend Louis. He knew that he had to learn about what he was up against, if he was to crack the scene. ***

One-night Smiley and Phil, went to the International Ballroom together to watch the Royal Showband performing. Brendan Boyer stood singing to a packed audience. A ten-piece band with clarinets, saxophones and trumpets stood behind him. Boyer sings 'The Hackleback'

Do the Hucklebuck, do the Hucklebuck, Wiggle like an eel, waddle like a duck.

The crowd were wild, shaking and dancing to the music. Brian and Phil stand at the bar.

-God help Ireland. Is this what we're up against? I've never seen so many 'gob-shites' in one place. How are we going to crack the scene? Said Phil.

***

A few weeks later Smiley managed to get, Phil a gig at the Ghetto Club. Just as they were loading up their van to leave, another van drove up. A show band boy, leans out the window. One of them started shouting.

-We want show-band music, not rock and roll.

-Rock and roll is here to stay. Shouts Phil.

***

Phil, invited a local girl named Claire, to the Star Cinema in Crumlin. She arrived dressed as a goth, with long black hair and tattoos on her arms. She had purple eye shadow and pink lipstick.

The film showing is "Easy Rider" starring Peter Fonda and Dennis Hopper.

-What's this film, then? asked Claire.

-Easy Rider. I hear it's a great movie about a biker.

***

On the big screen, Peter Fonda speeds down the highway on his bike. The song "Born to be Wild" drifts across the audience. Phil put his hand down the front of Claire's blouse. She slaps him sharply.

-Phil, please. She whispers.

He tries to kiss her on the neck. Suddenly an old beer bottle came flying across the cinema, just missing Phil's head.

-He nearly got me! Said Phil a little nervous.

-Are you ok?

-Let's get outa here Phil, its bleedin' dangerous in here.

***

Phil recovers and is sent home. One evening

he's in his flat chilling out in his bedroom. He gets up and searches under his bed. Finding a little box, he opens it. He takes out a lump of hash and starts rolling a joint. Lighting up, he puts on a Rolling Stones album. His Gran opens the door.

What's that queer smell round here?

-Aftershave, Gran

-It'd kill an elephant. I have a letter from your mother.

-I haven't heard from her in weeks. Don't tell her about me being beaten up!

-No, don't worry.

Phil opens the letter and starts reading it.

-She's invited me over to Manchester.

-Great, you don't see her enough Phil.

Phil picks up his guitar and hits the cords. The sound of the electric guitar booms out through the open window to whole housing estate.

A woman opposite leans out of the window and shouts.

-When are you going' ta cut out your bleedin racket! 'Me bleedin' 'husband's on nights'.

Phil leans out of the window.

-I'm just practising missus,

-Wait till I see your 'effin' auld fella.

-I don't have one.

Phil slams the window shut. Peter comes in.

Sounds great Phil, keep it up.

We need a place to jam.

-What's been going on?

-Some auld one, giving me a hard time, across the street.

-Don't worry, I'll take care of that, you just keep playing.

What can you expect? They've never heard an electric guitar before round here. Come on and watch the TV.

There's a gig on I want you to see.

***

Phil and Peter sit watching TV, cans of beer in their hands. The television flickers to show the crowd at the Isle of Wight Festival. Hendrix is playing - If six were nine.

-It's Jimmy Hendrix!

-That's right. Hendrix the King.

-I've never seen him play.

-Do you know something, Philo, you look like him. Hendrix struts across the stage wearing a headband; giving all he's got.

He's dynamite! Just look at the guitar playing.

Hendrix kneels, pulling the guitar strings with his tongue.

He rolls the guitar round his back, gets up and plays it above his shoulders. The crowd go wild.

-It's fucking great.

-You could play like him,

-He's the business, grins Phil, enthralled.

***

Outside the Dublin ballroom, hangs a sign, proudly painted in green and white.

"Dublin Ballroom Dancing Competition."

Inside Claire wears a flowing ballroom dress. She dances the tango with a tall, handsome young man. A number is tacked to her back. They have just finished when Phil comes in. Claire kisses him on the cheek.

-How's it going? Haven't seen you in ages.

Claire's dancing partner walks over to another girl.

-Who's he?

-He's my dancing partner. Don't be jealous, Phil, he's just a friend. Where've you been anyway? You haven't called round.

I've been busy with the band.

I've been busy too.

Claire sits down beside him. Phil kisses her. Getting carried away, they end up in a passionate embrace. He runs his hands down her leg and falls off the chair. A bouncer comes over and catches Phil by the scruff of the neck, dragging him to the main doorway. He's flung out onto the main street where he falls flat on his face.

***

The next day Phil's back in his bedroom and starts jamming, trying to imitate his new idol. The noise is enough to crack glass. There are banging noises outside. He opens the window and peers out. A fat man in a string vest, is outside his front door, looking upwards.

-I've been working all shagging night. I can't get any bleedin sleep. Will you shut that thing off?

-It's not a thing, it's a guitar. Phil shouts back.

He slams down the window. He hurries downstairs and opens the door.

A police officer is standing beside the fat man.

-Mr Philip Lynott?

-Yes, how can I help you?

I've had a number of complaints from the people on the street. You're creating a disturbance and breaking the peace. You'll have to cut it out, otherwise I'll be forced to arrest you.

-I've nowhere else to play.

-Get yourself a garage, or a bedsit in Rathmines. Anywhere but Crumlin. It's not a place for that kind of music, if that's what you call it.

-Your too old to understand.

-Now none of that. Said the policeman.

-It shouldn't be allowed; ordinary decent folk can't sleep with that gurrier around.

-Phil slams the door shut.

***

Later on, Phil is in uncle Pete's sitting room. He puts a record on.

-Listen to this, Phil it's by a black soul artist.

Phil listens intensely.

-It's your music, Phil it's the black man's music. This is the stuff you've got to listen to.

Pete takes out the record collection. The floor is strewn with records covers, The Yardbirds, The Who and The Animals.

-Look at this shit, it's fantastic!

Yeah, but nobody beats Hendrix. Said Phil.

You're right, but you could become the Irish Hendrix and get out of Crumlin.

Phil's brother, uncle Tim, arrives. Phil is busy listening to Jimmy Hendrix.

-Hey, Philip, how's it going? What's that you've got on?

-Jimi Hendrix. Where have you been?

-Up north side, working.

-So you're back in Crumlin?

-Well, I pay the rent round here.

-I've been hearing complaints from the neighbours about your new guitar. You're not going to end up

like that waster of a brother of mine, are you?

-Why not? It beats skinnin chickens.

-The boys at work don't believe it. I'm working my arse off, while you're playing rock and roll.

-Well, you know what they say around Crumlin, give us rock and roll, not dole.

-I know what they'll be saying to you, if they can't get any sleep round here.

Don't worry, Timmy, I'm jamming down at the Ghetto club and I'm getting my own gaff.

-Your own flat! What about your own home?

***

On Rathmine's Road, the clock in the clock tower strikes mid-day. Phil and his friend,

Brian Downey, walk into a large Georgian house.

-It's not the bleedin' Ritz, but it's a good place to crash. Said Phil.

-We can have some great parties at last Phil.

-Let's just have some fun, while we're here, howz about a Shaggin house warming? ***

Phil holds his first house warming. It all starts in the afternoon and by early evening the flat is packed with local heads and groupies. Brush is there with his band, Skid Row. "Riders on the Storm" by the Doors blares out of the stereo.

-Into this world were thrown.

Like a dog without a bone.

A Texan with long hair and a wide brimmed cowboy hat walks up to Phil and Brush and sticks out his hand.

The name's Big Lee. I'm from Texas. I heard that you're putting a band together, boys. What's it called? - The Orphanage.

-Well that's the best God damned name for a rock band I've ever heard!

-What are you doing over here?

-Oh, I'm rocking around Europe, checking out the scene.

-What kind of rock do you like?

-The Stones, The Beatles, Hendrix.

-Hendrix is King.

-No, Hendrix is God. Said Phil.

-Big Lee starts rolling a joint. Claire hurries up to Phil.

-Phil, the pigs are here!

A wave of panic circulates round the room. People start exiting through the back door.

Minutes later the drug squad arrives, sirens blaring.

The police break into the flat to find a room empty except for a lone drunk lying on the floor.

***

GI Joe and Big Lee hurry down a back alley, followed by Phil, Brian and Claire. The police run after them.

They catch Big Lee and hand cuff him. G.I. Joe jumps on his motor bike and tries to escape. But they catch him and arrest him. Phil and Claire jump in a taxi and make a getaway.

***

They find coke and has on Big Lee and GI Joe.

Big Lee and GI Joe are marched into Mountjoy Prison. Macker and Phil stand outside, watching sadly.

-We'll have to get them out.

***

Inside the gaol, G. I. Joe talks to one of his wardens.

-Hey, man, you can't do this to me, I'm an American.

-Where's your passport?

-It was stolen, man, I'm innocent. Look, I'm gonna crack up in here. The last time I was locked up was in Nam. I'll get nightmares in here.

-Well you get a free meal and a bed, what more could you ask

for'?

-Are there any rats here?

-Lots, but they ain't got four legs.

-Man you don't understand, when I see a rat I go ape shit, it happened in Nam, you don't understand.

-Look, Joe, just keep your mouth shut and you'll be out of here in a few months. You will be a celebrity round here. You're the first real live cocaine dealer we've caught in Ireland. The gaoler gave Joe a smile and walks away. Joe kicks his tin cup across the cell. ***

G.I. Joe is lying in his cell. The moonlight glows through the bars, water drips from the tap. Joe dreams of Vietnam. A B 52 bomber drops bombs. A helicopter filled with troops lands in the jungle. Palm trees swirl around. Another helicopter speeds over rice fields. Innocent victims lay dead, while villages burn. President Nixon talks about Vietnam on TV. A BF2 bomber drops bombs, destroying jungle villages. A helicopter filled with troops lands in the jungle. Palm trees swirl around. Another helicopter speeds over rice fields. Innocent victims lay dead, while villages burn.

A Vietcong solider holds a gun to Gi. Joes head. A rat cage is tied round his neck, while a rat eats his skull. G.I. Joe screams. Helicopters fly over the tropical forests. The rat's teeth are covered in blood. G.I. Joe wakes up in bed, screaming.

***

Claire stands waiting in the corridor of the Apollo in Crumlin. Phil's finishes his gig. He appears, surrounded by a crowd of girls.

-Where've you been? asks Claire.

-I've been busy.

Phil pushes his way through the crowd and enters an alleyway. Claire follows him. They stand facing each other, their eyes shining in the moonlight.

-What's wrong? asks Phil.

-We're wrong!

-What do you mean?

-We are two different people, I have no time, I have to spend more time with the band.

He walks away from her. She stares at his back, stunned.

***

Phil lays in his bed in the dark. His eyes closed. He begins to dream about his childhood. He is ten years old. He sees Brian running down the street. They are both wearing short pants. Phil has a catapult. He aims it at some milk bottles and breaks one.

-Good shot, Phil. Let me try.

Phil gives Brian the catapult. He aims and knocks another bottle over.

-I found a guitar. Really, it's in the dump.

The two boys jump over a wall. Beyond them is a giant rubbish dump. Brian climbs to the top of it. He finds what he's looking for, a broken guitar. He lifts it up.

-Great.

-It's got no strings, but I can fix it.

Phil and Brian have their photos taken in a phone booth. Phil tears them in half and gives some to Brian. They enter a church. Inside, they both kneel down to pray. Phil looks up at a statue of an angel with rows of candles. A priest comes along and sits down beside them.

-How are Philip and Brian today?

-Fine father.

Phil looks up at the angel.

-Can angels really fly?

-Yes, they can. When we die, they carry us up to heaven.

-When I die will they carry me up too?

-Yes, they will!

-Does God only love, white children.

-No, Philip, we are all God's children. It doesn't matter if you're black or white. It's the colour of your soul that matters. There are many white men with black souls.

-Isn't that right, Brian?

-Yes, father.

-God loves us all, there is darkness in the world, we must bring light into it. The priest takes a book out of his pocket and starts reading a poem. It's "The little Black Boy" by William Blake.

-My mother bore me in the southern wild,

And I am black, but, oh, my soul is white;

White as an angel is the English child… ***.

Phil and Brian go to the Ghetto Club, to practice on their guitar and drums. Brian begins to get impatient with Phil.

-We've got to get it right for Mc Gonagles, Phil. You're

Not hitting the right chords. Try again.

Phil tries again.

-That sounds great. Let's try a Stones' number.

They play `Satisfaction' together in complete harmony.

***

The next evening, they play at the Mc Gonagles.

Brian gives it all he's got. Phil struts about the stage.

There is a projection of an eight milli-metre film of nudes floating across the wall. The sound of exploding smoke bombs echoes around the hall. ***

A week later Phil and Brian are sit outside Zhivago's night club in Baggot St, drinking a pint.   They hear the song by Gilbert O'Sullivan singing 'Alone Again, Naturally'. Phil spots a beautiful girl with long dark hair and wearing a purple red dress. She smiles at him. Beads and jewellery dangle around her neck. Phil strolls up to her and sits down beside her.

-What's your name?

-Lizzy.

-Where are you from?

-I'm Irish, but my father was from south America. - Do you want to come inside Zhivagos?

-I'd love to.

-I'm a fan of yours, I've been to one of your gigs.

-Did you see me in Mc Gonagles?

-Yeah, you were were great!

-You're a real rocker, Lizzy.

-Nice one, Phil. Who's your friend? Said Brian.

-This is Brian Downey. He's my new drummer.

-I'll be your biggest fan ever, Phil.

***

They sit together, drinking beer inside the club.

-Here, guys, have a look at this!

Brian turns on a film projector. One of Andy Warhol's psychedelic films flashes across the wall. Images of the Empire State building appear.

-That's where it's at, boys.

The Velvet Underground plays in the background.

-Brian's right, says Phil. We've got to listen to other sounds, other influences, but Hendrix is where it's at for me.

-This Warhol crap is too spaced out. I want to keep the hard rock sound. Phil and Lizzy roll a joint and pass it round.

Lizzy puts on Van Morrison's "Astral Weeks." We hear Ballerina.

-It's Van the Man's "Astral Weeks." Have you heard it?

-He's a genius.' I wish I had a voice like him. I'd love to be a soul singer. The lyrics drift over them.

-Spread your wings, come on fly awhile Straight to my arms, little angel child.

-I feel like a stranger in this world, said Phil.

-Phil, you're always staring into space. Lizzy nudges him. Sometimes I feel I don't belong here, I'm screwed up, Lizzy.

-I'm a little black boy and I don't know my place.

-Phil, you don't know your place?

-I heard there were black Irish in the Caribbean, called Murphy and Malone's. They say the Irish have a lot in common with the blacks. Lizzy laughs.

-Well, maybe that's where you should be heading for Phil.

-The Irish were the first slaves to pick cotton in America.

-Well I can't see you picking cotton Philo. Said Lizzy,

putting her arm round him and kissing him on the cheek.

***

The next day Phil's is outside his flat in Rathmines. His bags are being thrown out on the street by the landlord.

-I don't want to see you around here again, you black Bastard!

Phil picks up his guitar and struts down the street, giving him the two fingers sign. *** Phil goes down to Bewley's in Grafton Street and meets Brian Downey.

-I lost the pad Brian, the landlord threw me out. We need a place to jam as well.

-They can crash in my place. Look the nuns in Eccles Street have a place to rent. The

Artane boys practice there. I used to play with them when I was a kid.

-The nuns? You can't be serious?

***

Phil leaves his gear behind the counter at Bewley's and heads for Eccles Street, with Brian.

The Artane Boys Band march down Eccles Street in full uniform, playing "The Minstrel Boy."

-The Ministrel Boy,

To the war has gone,

In the ranks of death, you will find him.

Back inside the convent, Phil walks down the corridor, his guitar is slung over his shoulders. Photos of The Artane Boys Band are pinned to a notice board with, with photos of orphans. Underneath is the label "Irish Orphans sent to America, 1896." ***

Minutes later Phil enters the practice room with Brian. They both hear the sound of a band passing under the window. One of the boys knocks on the door. Phil opens it. A young boy stands there, holding a trumpet.

57

-How's it going, what's your name? - Paddy, want to hear my trumpet.

-You can audition when you get a bit older. Wanna jam?

Paddy nods at him.

-Ok, can you play the "The Minstrel Boy?

-Yes I can!

Paddy finds his confidence. He lifts the trumpet to his lips and blows into it. Phil stands leaning against the wall, his arms folded, he is impressed by Paddy's performance.

***

Phil goes to Mountjoy Prison to visit G.I. Joe.

-You've got to get me out of here, Phil, I'm going crazy.

-When's the case coming up?

-Two months - What about bail?

-Two thousand quid.

-Jasus! That's a lot!

-Look, Phil, get me out of here, man. It's Vietnam all over again. I'm having nightmares.

I'll see what I can do.

***

The next day Phil walks into the Garda station. He signs a bail order and puts two thousand pounds on the table.

***

G.I. Joe is lying in his cell at Mountjoy Prison. The jailer came and opened the door.

-Your time's up.

-What do you mean?

-Someone paid your bail.

Big Lee bail is also paid by Phil.

Phil sits waiting outside in Big Lee's pink Cadillac.

***

A few days later Phil goes down to Dino's Bar for a burger. Brian is there, with a beer in his hand.

-Any gigs coming up? asks Phil.

-Yeah, we got one.

-It's a fancy dress party. A Venetian masked ball. Yeah, it's at Trinity college, for all the toffs.

-Were the support act.

-Support act!

-Yeah some Beatles act called Sergeant Pepper, is the main act.

-You can't be serious!

-I think we found a new band member. His names Eric, he should be here soon. A long curly haired rocker enters the café and approaches them He carries an electric guitar.

Hello, my name's Eric Bell.

-You sound like a northerner.

-I 'm from Belfast.

-What brings you down here?

-I'm with the Dreams Show band. I'm really pissed off with the band scene.

-Yeah, it's a pain in the arse.

-How about putting a band together?

-I have a band. The Orphanage.

-Yeah, but I want to put together a real rock and roll band.

-Your band called the Orphanage, it's not a good name.

-Have you any ideas, said Phil.

Lizzy enters the café.

-Hi, Lizzy, this is Eric.

-Hiya Eric, Brian how are you?

-We are trying to think of a new name for the band. We have a gig in Trinity College.

Phil looks at Lizzy.

-Lizzy that's it, we will call it after you.

Lizzy, how about Thin Lizzy, it's a tin robot in the Beano comic.

-They called me Thin Lizzy in school, I was bullied a lot.

-That's it, great name. Said Eric.

-Phil, that really cool, I love it. Lizzy said kissing him.

-You know what the problem it's the show bands, they control the whole scene.

-Yeah, but is Ireland really ready to rock?

-Course it is; they just haven't heard us yet? - But no Irish rock band has ever made it by playing, Mc Gonagles and The Baggot.

-You're right; we gotta hit England, then America. - How can we go anywhere on thirty-five quid a gig?

-We can get more on the ballroom circuit. Anyway that's not our problem, we need a manager.

-I know a guy called Terry O'Neill, he'll manage us.

-Is he straight, can we trust him?

-Of course we can.

We need a keyboard player. Said Phil.

-I know on,his names Eric like me. Eric Wrixton.

-Two Erics in a band, that's going to confuse us all!

***At the Trinity Ball in the Buttery Bar, students are dressed for a Venetian masked ball. Many of the girls are scantily clad, some are dressed as French maids. There are large breasted transsexuals strutting about in high heels. Others wear seventeenth century wigs and long, false eyelashes. One girl flashes a garter. Many wear Venetian masks.

Phil looks over to the stage, where a band are setting up.

On the drum is written 'Sergeant Pepper's Lonely Hearts Club'.. The band members are all dressed in psychedelic gear, Beatles style from the album.

-Where are you boys from?

-Liverpool.

-You look like the real thing.

-We are, we were around long before the Beatles, I knew

John Lennon, when he was a kid. I taught him how to play the guitar.

What's the Sergeant Pepper connection?

-Well, we're the original band but no one believes us.

-My names Harry Pepper, they call me Sergeant Pepper. I gave John the idea for the album.

They made it and we didn't, that's rock and roll.

■■■■■■■■■■■■■■■■■■■■■■■■■■■■■■■■■■■■■■

Terry O'Neill, the prospective manager, is invited back stage to the dressing room. They shake hands warmly.

-Phil how's it going?

-We just gotta get a tour together,

-Let me sort out the ballroom scene. Some of them don't like rock bands. - No problem! We're ready.

-It's a tough game Phil, no Irish rock band has ever made it big.

-We're stuck on this bleedin island. You got to think of England and America, that's where to aim for.

-It's like backing a horse. We've got big odds against us.

-I know, but we can do it. The Irish have got guts; we can play sounds the punters have never heard before.

***

Later that evening, Phil and Lizzy, lie together on the lawn in Trinity College. The moon shines down

through the trees, making patterns on Lizzy's leopard-skin coat as they kiss.

-I love you Phil. Thank you for naming the band after me. I hope it become the biggest band in the world!

-I hope so to!

***

The next week Phil gets back to rehearsing at the convent. He sits strumming his guitar and sing one of his new lyrics.

Lizzy walks in.

-Phil! There you are!

She looks round.

-What a bleedin' place.

-Did the nuns let you in?

-They're a right bunch of weirdos.

-Like yourself, Lizzy.

-Like you, Philo? What are you up to?

-Putting some songs together. I've got a song called the Rocker. - How does it go?

-I'm your man, if you're looking for trouble I'll take no lip. If I kicked your face you'd be seeing double.

Lizzy laughs.

-You really fancy yourself, Philo. I suppose you think you're gonna be the new Elvis. They'll be calling you the

Crumlin rocker.

-Lizzy you always take the piss. It's all a big joke to you, isn't it?

-Well, you don't meet many rock-stars in Dublin these days.

-Listen to this new song I wrote; it's called 'Little

Black Boy.'

-I'm a little black boy, and I don't know my place.

-Philo, that's right, you don't know your place.

She laughs. Phil kisses her.

-Phil, what about the nuns?

Outside a nun is passing along the corridor. She stands outside, listening. She looks up to heaven, she makes the sign of the cross and then walks on.

***

The next day Terry is at an agent's office. The agent sits, smoking a cigar.

-I don't like rock bands, they're too noisy. The punters want the show bands. Dicky Rock, Brendan Boyer and Big Tom. They want a few pints, and good auld Dublin mott.

-But things are changing, the kids are into Top of the Pops and buying rock albums.

-This is Ireland, not England or America, remember. It's an island of saints and scholars. It run by a bunch of mullahs, called priests. - Rock is going to catch on.

-Maybe, but the clergy don't like this rock and roll, it's too promiscuous.

-But the kids love this stuff.

The agent laughed.

-Alright, then, I'll give you one gig with a show band. If the public don't want it, you're out. What's your band called.

-Thin Lizzy!

***

Inside a nightclub a show bands performs with trumpets, base players and pianists. A man in a blue suit stands singing, "A Long Way to Tipperary." Phil and

Brian and Eric, look on from the wings.

-What a load of old crap. Said Eric.

-Well, it shouldn't be hard to compete with that lot.

The blue suited man finishes his piece and the announcer comes on stage.

-And now we're going to hear a new band, ladies and gentlemen, please give a welcome to Thin Lizzy!

The boys walk on and play, starting with "The Rocker." Phil belts out the song.

The audience go wild. Girls scream as Phil struts across the stage. He starts to sing, "I'm a Little Black Boy, with Brian on drums and Eric on guitar.

Phil gyrates his hips and the girls go wild.

Later Phil is in the dressing room with the band. GI Joe arrives with Big Lee.

-Phil man, how's it going. Said Gi Joe, throwing his arms around him.

-Ok man, it great to be out? No rats! Mice but no rats.

-I love your gig, you guys have come on a lot since you started. said Big Lee.

***

Afterwards the band celebrated with a party in Mackers flat.

The drink flows. Phil has his arms round Lizzy.

-You were just great, Phil.

Phil takes out a mirror and a piece of silver paper.

-What's that, Macker gave it to me, after the gig.?

-Coke let's try some.

Phil takes the powder out and runs a blade along the mirror. Lizzy rolls a pound note and begins to snort.

-C'mon Lizzy, try some.

-It's not for me.

-Go on.

Phil snorts the coke. The room begins to blur. Colours and faces swirl around.

***

Phil wakes up lying in an alleyway. He sees a police officer standing over him.

-You're in a sorry state.

-Where am I?

-Baggot Street.

-Wher's Lizzy.?

-Lizzy, who is Lizzy?

-How did I get here?

-You tell me.

Phil staggers to his feet, making his way down the alleyway.

***

A few nights later, Phil and the boys are doing another

gig in a ballroom. Phil stands belting out;

'Dedication', to a packed audience. The crowd go crazy. Terry stands talking to an agent.

-It's hot stuff.

-Never thought this music would catch on.

-It's sex and drugs and rock and roll. If that's what they want, we'll give it to them. Phil has the x factor, he's the new Hendrix, or maybe the new Elvis.

***

After the gig Phil goes walking Sandymount beach with Lizzy.

-Phil, what happened to Claire?

-I Just wasn't into her.

-Maybe you'll drop me too.

-Let's not get so heavy. Lizzy. I like you, let's leave it at that.

-That's not good enough.

-Oh Phil, you're impossible.

-Lizzy, give us a break. I don't know what commitment means, my father never gave my mother any commitment.

-Why not?

-He just disappeared.

-So you never had a father. Is that really important to you?

-Sometimes, I think about him. I dream about meeting him.

-Just forget him. Relationships come and go.

Can love last forever?

-I don't know Phil, maybe.

-What about you, Lizzy? You never talk about yourself.

-I grew up in London and came over here when I was fifteen. Your father, mother, where are they?

-My father went back to South America.

-And your mother?

-She lives in England. I got my gran and my two uncles, Timmy and Pete. They are like family to me. I was brought up by my aunt.

-But Phil, what happened to your father?

-I am not sure he was from Guyana in South America. If my father loved my mother, why didn't he stay?

Maybe I was just an accident.

-So what's your big dream?

-I don't want to be stuck in some two quid an hour job, skinning chickens. Crumlin people work hard, but it's a tough life there for people, stuck in their council flats.

-So you don't want the house with two kids?

I don't know, but I do want a record deal and a hit in the charts.

-Do you really think an Irish rock band can make it?

-I'm not sure, no Irish band has ever made it big before.

Maybe I'm a dreamer.

-And why not!

-You need guts and a lot of luck and some good tracks. The music business is cut-throat.

-I know you have guts, Phil, but do you have what it takes?

Phil kisses her.

-Music is all I've got!

***

The next night Brian and Phil talk in The Bailey.

-We've got a recording deal.

-With who?

-With John Dardis, but he wants us to record his song.

It's called 'I Need You'.

-Great! Another ego maniac!

Well it's like the song, he doesn't need us, we need him.

-I've got a song called "The Farmer." - We'll put it on the other side.

***

Later on, Phil's on stage with a brass band, trombones and a saxophonist. Phil sing the song.

'Don't Believe a Word'

Don't believe me if I tell you. Especially if I tell you that I'm in love with you.

The girls go wild and some of them try to climb on stage.

***

A few hours later and Phil's in his dressing room. He sits strumming his guitar. Terry comes in.

-How did the single go?

-It bombed, we need a new record deal.

Phil snorts some coke.

-Not now Phil, you're playing this gig soon.

-Look, Terry, I need the stuff.

-I don't like you on the stuff. It'll burn you out.

I don't care. I need it. It gives me energy.

-We need a record deal; we can't survive on fifty quid a gig.

-Did you hear the news?

-What news?

-Hendrix is dead.

Phil looks shocked.

-Dead! Hendrix.

-It was an overdose, heroin. - He was so good.

***

Later on Phil's sits having a drink at the Bailey with Lizzy. Eric and Brian arrive.

-Have you heard?

-Heard what?

-Terry has sold Lizzy for a hundred and fifty quid.

-A hundred and fifty quid? Lizzy - our band? That's all we're worth.

-A hundred and fifty quid! Where's Terry?

-He split - can't find him.

***

The next day, Phil and Brian are practicing in the recording studio.

-We need a bleedin hit if we want to crack London.

-No Irish band has ever made it that big.

-Sounds good.

***

It's the early hours of the morning. The band are all back at Phil's flat. Macker puts some coke on a mirror. Big Lee pours some whisky.

-Have some of the Irish dew.

-It's the hard stuff.

-I've got harder stuff.

What's that?

Big Lee opened a bottle.

-Hard stuff. Try Chinese whiskey.

-Chinese Whiskey!

Dead mice could be seen swirling around the bottle.

-We drank it in Nam, you just put a few dead mice in it and let it sit for few days.

-Dead mice!

-Yeah, it gives it the extra bite. Hold on, I got another trick up my sleeve.

G.I. Joe walks over to a bucket near the kitchen sink. He reaches in and takes out a long eel then nails it to the wall. The eel's head spurts with blood. G.I. Joe runs a blade down its back. He gets a whisky glass and catches the flowing blood. Phil looks on in amazement.

-That's what I call a Bloody Mary!

To everybody's amazement, G.I. Joe guzzles down all the whisky.

Phil walks out of the bar alone. Out in the empty Dublin Street, he holds his head low, feeling as though he has lost a brother. He walks into the Five Club and sits drinking whisky and playing Hendrix on the jukebox. Brian arrives.

-I got a call just an hour ago. We've got a deal with Decca, in London.

-Great! At last we're heading for the top!

***

At Dun Laoghire Harbour, the Thin Lizzy van arrives. Hundreds of people are getting on board, an emigrant ship They are all crossing the Irish sea, to England. Lizzy's comes with him to say goodbye. Phil stands on deck and waives back, smiling sadly.

***

A few hours later, they arrive in Holyhead. They speed down the motorway towards Manchester and arrive outside the Clifton Grange hotel. Phil jumps out, as his mother rushes down the steps.

-It's great to see you, mother.

-And how's my son, Phil? I see you got an afro. - Meet the band, mam, this is Brian and Eric.

-Pleased to meet you Mrs Lynott. Said Brian.

-Me too. Said Eric.

-Call me Philomena!

-Come on in, boys, you must be starving.

***

Phil, Eric and Brian have a drink at the bar. A tall, blonde, trans-sexual walks in and sits on the bar stool next to Phil. Phil is surprised be this new encounter.

-This is Mavis, she's an actress.

-Well, I've been on stage a few times.

-This is my son, Philip and his friends, Eric and Brian,

-Well, I can hardly say he's the spitting image of you.

-His father was a black south American, his family was brought over with the slave trade.

Well, Phil I'll have to show you around Manchester one night. There are some great tranny clubs round here.

-We don't have many trannies in Ireland.

-What are you talking about? There are loads of men running around in skirts, called priests.

We've gone up market recently, haven't we, Mavis? - We have that, I only let rooms out to celebrities, actors and musicians and the like. We're into the glamour business now, Phil. - Is Percy still around?

-Yes, he is Phil, he's still in that room in the attic, still playing his guitar. She lifts the hotel phone and presses a button.

-Is that you, Percy? I've got somebody here to see you.

Why don't you come down to the bar to join us? A few minutes later a Bibi King look-alike walks in, carrying a guitar.

Well if it isn't Philip! Why, the last time I saw you I bought you an ice cream. Phil throws his arms around the grinning Percy.

-Percy taught me how to play the guitar!

-I still have that same guitar! I bought it for five dollars in Texas twenty years ago. Percy, meet the band. This is Eric and Brian.

A band indeed! Well you always wanted to be a rock star.

-And I always said to you that there was only one man in my life and that was Woody Guthrie.

-We gotta get together for a jammin' session. I wanna see how you've got on. ***

That night Phil sat in the hotel lounge with his mother.

-I just heard from your father last week. Would you like to meet him?

-I've always wanted to.

-He's in London.

-I'm not sure how I'm gonna feel when I meet him. One part of me wants to see him but the other part feels rejected and abandoned.

We all make decisions in life that seems right at the time. Your father had his problems, you got to understand that.

-I can't understand how a father abandons his son and

Then wants to see him thirty years later, it doesn't make sense.

-Maybe its old age and guilt.

-Well, we'll just have to see, we're gonna be busy, it's a fantastic break coming over here.

-I know, I'm just so proud of you.

Tears start to fall from her eyes, as she embraces him.

-Phil, it's good to see you? I've been so worried.

-I was in love with your father.

-But, what happened?

-Some people just grow apart. You know, Phil, I wanted to talk to you about what happened.

-I've always wondered. I was upset recently when I heard this story circulating that I was left barefoot and pregnant on some dockside by a sailor.

-I thought that was the story.

No, no, it wasn't like that, people twist things round. It's not the truth. I loved him, but we just grew apart. We were so different.

-I've always felt like an orphan abandoned.

-I didn't want to go to England but we were so poor in those days. This was Ireland of the fifties. I had no money and I was pregnant. Do you know what it was like to be pregnant outside marriage in those days?

-What was it like?

-Terrible, really bad. There was a big stigma about it - Catholic Ireland - such hypocrisy. So I let your grandmother look after you. I could have ended up in the Magdalene laundry or forced to adopt you. I went to England and sent what money I could. I felt you would have a better life here than in England, so stop thinking of yourself as an orphan. I love

You, we all love you. I felt I was doing the right thing.

Please forgive me. She rubs her hands together nervously. Phil gets up and kisses his mother on the forehead.

-I love you too, ma.

***

Phil says good bye to his mother. She gives him his father's phone no. Phil and the band, head for the recording studio in London. They sit listening to the sound mix. The sound engineer smiles and gives them a thumbs up.

-Great! We'll have it out in twenty-four hours.

-Fantastic. Here's hoping we get some cash soon.

-Have you got a place to crash?

-No, we're broke.

-I know the King of the Hippies, Sid Rawle, he's up in Chalk Farm. He's turned his whole street into squats. The houses are all painted with rainbows and

everything's laid on for free, no rent and loads of women, booze and as much dope as you want.

-Sounds great.

-Just turn up and tell him I sent you. Chicken Fisher's the name.

***

The band cruise down to Chalk Farm in the van, until they find Hippy Valley.

-Well, the rainbows are there, let's give it a shot. Said Phil.

Maybe this is paradise.

Phil, Eric and Brian get out of the van and approaches a door surrounded by paintings of giant sunflowers. He pulls on a rope. A giant bell overhead rings out.

The door opens. A beautiful blonde haired girl with pink mascara and flowers around her neck answers the door.

-My name's Phil, this is Brian and Eric. We have a band called Thin Lizzy. Chicken Fisher sent me here to see Sid Rawle.

-Sid's on the phone to New York, come on in. Phil and the boys enter in awe. The walls are covered with pictures of Buddha and there are candles burning.

They enter a large room. Sid is lying on a cushion while three beautiful girls sit on settees smoke joints and listen to music. He motions them to sit down on the floor while he speaks.

-Things are going well over here, John. That last twenty

thousand dollars went towards buying Dawlish Island for our hippy colony, off the coast of Ireland.

How's Yoko?

Phil turns to Eric and whispers.

-Is that who I think it is?

-John Lennon!

-Well, John it sounds like you're really bored and homesick. Don't forget you're always welcome here we got a spare room for you.

You may say I'm a dreamer but I'm not the only one, sounds like the lyrics for a good song. Listen, man I've gotta go. Catch you later love to Yoko.

Sid puts the phone down.

-What can I do for you man?

-Chicken Fisher sent us here. We have a band called Thin Lizzy. We need a place to crash. This is Brian and Eric my names Phil. Was that who I think it was?

-Yep, it sure is, that's the famous John Lennon - he supports our cause. Rising rents, prices on houses and flats, England has gone mad.

-We're recording an album with Decca.

-No problem. I'm trying to fill up all of the five hundred rooms, otherwise they'll get into disrepair.

-Five hundred rooms! That's incredible.

-If the government won't solve the homeless crisis, I'll give it a shot. We've got a political party called the

Rainbow Party. I'm working with screaming Lord Such, the leader of the Monster Raving Looney party. He

wants the government to bring over the E.E.C wine lakes to England and he's offering free skiing trips down E.E.C butter mountains. He's coming round this afternoon. Phil and the boys break into peals of laughter. Sid turns to the girls.

-This is Suzy Cadillac, Madison and Mabel.

-The girls smile.

-I took them off the streets in the sixties. Their mothers overdosed. They were into flower power.

Sid hears a horn bleeping. He gets up and walks towards the window.

Lord Such stepped out of a Rolls Royce.

-Look! It's Screaming Lord Sutch, Speak of the devil!

Madison, escorts him in. Sutch walks into the room in a leopard skin suit and hat.

-Good day to you all.

-Sutch, meet the Irish rock band, Thin Lizzy. This is Phil, Brian and Eric. You know the girls, don't you? So what brings you round?

-I'm on my way to the Bowie's Ziggy Stardust concert.

Want to come, boys and girls?

They all nod.

-So what kind of music do you play, boys?

-Rock and roll. Were from Dublin.

-Well, the music scene is far out over here. I've got a band called the Raving Savages. I climb in and out of coffins on stage and pour buckets of blood over the audience, that kind of thing. We'll have time to talk later. Come on folks, I've got the Rolls outside. They all pile into the Rolls.

-How's about this for a tin can? I bought it for two hundred quid from some toff, who was on cocaine. ***

They pull up outside the marquee. A large crowd is gathered outside. Sutch struts up to the bouncers.

-My name is Lord Sutch. Me and my mates are on the guest list.

-To everyone's amazement the bouncer nods approval.

***

Inside the marquee bar, Sutch orders champagne.

-I knew Bowie when we signed on at the same dole office in Brixton. Him and Ziggy.

-Ziggy!

-Ziggy was a bloke that wore all this crazy make up and gear, he was a local tranny who sang George Fornby songs on aukulele.

-I don't believe it, l thought Ziggy was just a made up fantasy figure.

-No he existed, He was even better than the real thing. They find their seats. The place is packed out. Bowie appears in an incredible silver suit, out of the

darkness and into the spotlight, performing Starman as Ziggy Stardust. Phil is stunned by the performance, Eric and Brian too.

-If you want to crack the music scene in London, that's what you're up against. ***

Phil read the name and number on the piece of paper his mother gave him. It reads - Cecil Parris Lynott.

Phil dials the number on Sid Rawles phone. Someone answers. It is Phil's father. Phil is nervous. He arranges to meet him in the Irish pub in Camden town. Two hours later Phil arrives there.

He sits nervously at the bar. He looks towards the door. The light streams through. A tall black man appears in a leather jacket. He wears beads around his neck and sports a handlebar moustache. He has faded jeans a cowboy boots with spurs.

He approaches Phil. He looks into his eyes and puts his hands around him.

-Phil my boy, my boy, it's so good to see you!

-Me too dad. I have waited a long time for our meeting.

-Have a beer.

-Mines a whiskey, Jack Daniels I need it!

-They sit and face the bar.

-Look Phil, I came to say that I am sorry about everything. Sorry I was not there for you. I tried to see you but it did not work out. I went back to south America. I was there many years.

-Ok OK dad, you don't have to say sorry. I understand.

-You see son, sometimes life does not work out the way you want. Been an emigrant here in London a'int easy. I came over on the Windrush ship from Jamaica. I arrived here in 1948, without a cent in my pocket. Along with me were four hundred and ninetythree other poor souls searching for a future. So it was tough.

-I forgive you dad. I forgive you for everything. I just hope we can see more of each other.

-You sure will son. Said his father swigging on his Jack Daniels.

-Thank you son, God bless you.

-Philomena tells me you have a band. Don't forget to invite me to one of your gigs.

-You have free tickets to all my gigs dad.

-I hope so and throw in a few free drinks too son.

***

Back in Ireland Lizzy is in a car with big Lee. They are parked on Sandymount Beach, looking out over the moonlit sea.

-I heard Kid Jensen, is pushing Phil's album.

-Let's try the channels.

Lizzy fiddles with the radio. There's a crackling noise and the sound of Kid Jensen comes over the air.

-We've got it.

-This is the Kid Jensen Show. Tonight we're playing one of the best albums around. It's like gold dust, from the new Irish band, Thin Lizzy.

The music soars across the waves.

-I heard that Jensen is playing the arse out of this album. He's really pushing it. It's reached number two in Radio

Luxembourg's Hot Heavy Top 20. Tonight we play Thin Lizzy's new release, "New Day." Lynott's song about Dublin. The music soars over the airways. -How can I leave the town, that brings me down, that has no jobs, is blessed by God and makes me cry, Dublin.

***

Back in Dublin in the Five Club, Big Lee sits at the bar. Skid Row are playing a gig. Macker, the drug dealer comes in.

-How's it going Brush?

Brush nods. Macker talks to Big Lee.

-Well if it ain't Macker.

-What's up, man?

-How's the buzz man?

-Are you dealin' around here tonight?

-What do you want? Speed, hash, uppers, downers?

-Throw few johnnies while you're at it.

What's the story here in Ireland?

-You can't get no supply here, it's kinda not allowed.

-What do you mean, not allowed?

-You've got to be married to get them. If you go down to the local doctor, he'll throw you out.

-You don't say?

That's right man, this is Catholic Ireland, you know what they say, there was no sex in Ireland before TV. But if you got cash baby, it's no problem.

-You must all be really frustrated around here.

-We all say our prayers, man.

-Here's fifty dollars- sort it out.

***

It is pitch dark. Macker and Big Lee, is outside the chemist's shop. He runs down an alleyway and climbs over a brick wall.

Smashing a window of a chemist shop with a brick, he breaks in. Inside the shop, he sees lines of drugs on the shelves.

He stuffs them into his pocket. The alarm goes off. They jump out the window. They hear blaring of sirens. A police car pulls up. The escape over the back wall.

***

The next day, Brush and some of the local heads, meet up at the Bailey. Phil walks in, Lizzy is there. They hug each other.

-Phil! It's great to see you!

-How are you? I've missed you, how was England?

-We were just so busy recording all the time.

-So the band's really going places. - Want to come to the Pink?

***

Phil and Lizzy sit inside the Pink Elephant Club, sipping their drinks.

-Dublin, I missed the place. When you grow up here you love and hate it. You want to get out, but when you leave you want to come back again. It's happened to so many artists, so many Irishmen sitting in bars across the world.

-Ireland is changing, you're changing it, Phil.

-Maybe, but I'm going to move to London. You can come with me.

-Of course. Have you been thinking of me?

-Of course.

-You have too many women now, Phil. Someday you'll realise you just want loyalty, maybe even love.

-I love you Lizzy, you're my baby. We named the band after you.

-Phil, I'll always be around. Said Lizzy kissing him.

-Have you any new songs?

-Yeah, I'm writing a song called "'Legend of the

Vagabond."

-What's it about?

-It's about a strange traveller from afar who meets and falls in love with a young girl, fathers a child and leaves on the night the child is born.

-It sound like your fathers, story.

-How does it go?

Phil takes out a piece of paper.

All male descendants of the fatherless child are blessed in the art of love, to win the heart of many, cursed never to be in love.

-You can't forget him, you're always thinking of him. - It must be difficult for you.

-Sometimes I feel it, an emptiness inside, something missing, as if I lost something a long time ago.

Lizzy kisses him.

-Well you found me.

***

The next day Phil's strolls down Crumlin, when Macker drives up on a motorbike.

-What do you think?

-It looks fab.

-Want a run?

Phil gets on the bike and they speed down the street.

-There's a party at the Hellfire Club, wanna come?

Big Lee coming too, he is right behind me!

At that moment Big Lee came along, driving a pink Cadillac.

-What do you think, Phil?

-It's great. Let's drive over and pick Lizzy up.
- Good idea, we need some women around.

***

Lizzy jumps into the back of the Cadillac. She sticks her head between Phil and Big Lee.

-It's really fab, Big Lee.

-Have you heard from G.I. Joe?

-Hes ok.

-Tell Joe when you see him I am writing a song about a gaol break.

***

They pull up outside the hellfire Club in the Wicklow Mountains. Some people are sitting on grass outside, drinking beer around a camp fire. They join the group.

In the distance glows the sparkling skyline of Dublin.

Lizzy turns to Phil.

-Let's go find some magic mushrooms.

-Where?

-Just follow me.

-Phil smiles at Big Lee and they all hurry off into the woods. They eventually come to a clearing where there are hundreds of magic mushrooms.

-There are hundreds! Lizzy starts to pick them. A giant stone, rises in the distance.

-What's that?

-It's the sacred stones, if you stand beneath them you'll never grow old. They walk towards the stones.

***

A photographer takes photos of three girls standing by the stones. They wear Celtic dresses and long Celtic shawls, which are wrapped around them. Lizzy recognises her friend.

-Jim! How's it going?

-Lizzy! Great to see you.

-This is the Jim Fitzpatrick; he does fantastic Celtic designs.

-This is Phil, he's got the new Thin Lizzy band. What are you up to?

-I'm taking some shots for a book cover.

-Phil needs an album cover.

-I'm into Celtic stuff and ancient Ireland, how about you?

-Yeah, Phil's into anything, rock, Celtic rock.

-Celtic rock.

-Well you could call it that.

-Can you do a cover for me.

-Sure.

***

At "The 5 Club" Phil and the Band are performing.

They perform Orphanage.' Big Lee arrives.

-I heard you're hitting the big time.

-We still need a major hit.

-You'll get there, boy. Just keep going. Here, have a pint.

***

Eric and Phil watch the news on television.

-Today there were several explosions in Talbot

Street.

101

Eric looks disturbed.

-I am really worried, Phil. What about my folks back in Belfast? Maybe I should get back to see them.

-We need you in the band, Eric. Stick around.

-Look let's go up to Belfast. We can do a few gigs there and I can check in on the ma and da.

-Great, I've never been up there.

-I'll get Terry to organise it.

*** Phil drinks with Eric Bell in O'Donoghue's Pub. A traditional Irish band is playing some tunes, called the Dubliners.

-Phil, that's a good song.

-Maybe it could rock it up.

-Maybe, it's real Celtic rock.

Luke Kelly starts bantering with the crowd around him and talks to Phil.

-Play us another. How about `Whiskey in the Jar'?

-No problem.

-They begin to play.

-As I was going over the Cork and Kerry mountains, I met Captain Farrell and the money he was counting.

I first produced my pistol and then produced my rapier…

-It's not a bad song.

-Go on Philo. Give it a blast on the electric. Yeah.

Phil takes his electric guitar out of his case and plugs it into to the sound system.

-It'll blow the place apart.

-Go on, give us a blast.

-O.K. If you want a blast, I'll give you a blast.

Phil opens the case, takes out the electric and plugged it into the amp without hesitation. He steps on a chair and onto the bar, to the amusement of everyone. He lets rip and plays 'Whiskey in the Jar `at full blast. Very soon, a crowd gathers outside, trying to get in. ***

The next day Lizzy is in her flat with Phil. She switches on the TV and watches the Larry Gogan Radio Show. Thin Lizzy appears on the screen, playing "Whiskey in the Jar."

-Irish rock has reached new thresholds with many new influences. Thin Lizzy rivals the rock sound of Hendrix and The Stones. New groups like Horslips and Tir Na Nog are bringing in Celtic influences, it's called Celtic Rock. Thin Lizzy has hit the English charts with `Whiskey in the Jar" reaching number six. They're on their way to pop stardom, certainly the most promising group in Ireland. ***

Back at Phil's house Phil's Gran is talks to uncle Pete.

-I'm proud. The whole of Crumlin is talking about him.

-It's a hit, an Irish traditional song, becoming a rock hit, incredible. You know, he's the first Irish rock star to make it into the British charts! Said Pete smiling.

***

The next day sees Phil and Brian talking outside a pub.

-Have you heard the news? Gary Moore, has dropped out of Skid Row.

-Brush must be pissed off.

-Skid row's breaking up.

-That's crazy, they're one of the best rock bands around.

-Well it's up to us now, Phil. How long are we going to keep this show on the road?

-Dunno. We'll have to hope.

They both walk into the pub where the radio announces.

-Tonight the IRA continued their bombing campaign in Belfast. There were several explosions.

-What's up Eric?

-Listening to all stuff about the bombing campaign, it's getting really bad.

-I'm worried about my family. I am worried about you too. Rock and roll, killed Jimi Hendrix, Jim Morrison and Janis Joplin. They all died of drug overdoses before their time.

-You gotta slow down Phil. Cut the drugs, find a steady woman. Forget all these groupies, they don't care about you. Stick with Lizzy, she loves you.

Phil switches on the radio.

-Today members of the Miami Band were murdered at the border.

-Jasus, Phil, they got the Miami. That's heavy man.

-What's happening to Ireland?

***

Brian and Phil are chilling out in Phil's flat.

-Phil you got to find a steady woman.

-Cut the drugs; find a good woman and hold on to reality,

-What about Lizzy?

-Yeah, Lizzy. I'm seeing her again. Brian starts strumming on his guitar - How's it going, Phil?

-I'm wrecked, was drinking with Brush, until the late hours

-What's that you're putting on?

-It's a video of the Sex Pistols at the Brixton Academy.

Great! Let's watch it!

Sid Vicious appears on the screen, singing a Frank Sinatra song.

-Poor old Frank Sinatra, must be turning in his grave.

-It's the new thing in Britain, it's real anarchy.

-He's doing it his way. He's off his head.

***

Phil walks down Grafton Street, bands are performing. There are flame throwers and jugglers. The Dice Man performs. Photographer Mark Begley takes photos. He walks up to the camera, his face painted white and stares in. Then he smiles and blows a kiss. Mick Mulcahy, a performance artist climbs up a lamp post, his clothes covered in paint. He shouts across the crowd.

-It's the revolution.

Fly to the moon with me.

The future is yours.

He climbs down and starts an Irish dance.

Phil sees a group of Hari Krishna's wearing robes and chanting

"Hari Krishna."

A middle aged man appears, wearing a billboard which reads-"Man has sinned against God." He walks up the the Krishnas and shouts at them.

-God will punish you! Repent! Repent!

The Krishna priest bows to him and hands him a flower.

-God, save Ireland!

Phil spots Macker in the crowd. He comes up beside him and takes some acid tabs out of his pocket and shows them to Phil.

-What are they?

-Acid man, like to try one?

Phil took one. Macker took one too.

Acid, is heaven, Phil remember, it's the road to paradise, man. let's go back to your flat.
***

Back in Mackers flat Phil pops one into his mouth.

Minutes later, Phil's world turns into a terrible nightmare. Macker's body metamorphoses into a giant bat, which stands snarling at him. The room is full of giant rats.

Phil goes to the window and climbs out onto the ledge. Macker calls out.

-Phil don't jump!

I'm not jumping. I'm going to fly.

Phil imagines himself flying through space. He plunges into the water, beneath him. He walks through some open doors. From there he finds himself in a long tree lined avenue. The light streams through the trees. An old black man stands before him. It was his dad!

-Is that you, Dad?

-It is Phil, I've come to say that I'm always with you.

I'm an angel by your side.

-I miss you, Dad.

I have to go away, but I'm always with you, Phil.

Phil wakes up in bed in a cold sweat. Macker stands in front of him, sweat pouring from his brow. ***

Two nights later sees Pete Short selling newspapers outside Bewley's cafe

-Read all about it, Dublin the city of - One Thousand Rock Bands, the revolution has begun!

Joe, the revolutionary, waives a red flag. On it is written - Give us Rock and Roll, not Dole!

-The revolution has begun! We can no longer stand idly by on the dole. Rock and roll will change Ireland.

I tell you comrades, rock and roll for the unemployed. Give us rock and roll, not dole.

***

The next day, Phil listens to the Larry Gogan show. - The scene is changing in Dublin, new influences are coming in to Ireland, especially punk. The Sex Pistols have made a big impact on the new rock scene, more that is more radical than ever. Watch out for new bands like; The Atrix,The Blades, Micro Disney, Some Kind Of Wonderful and The Radiators From Space.

***

That night Phil lays in bed in the Clarence Hotel listening to his song – Got to Give It Up.

"Now I've been messing with the heavy stuff and for a time I couldn't get enough. ***

The next morning Lizzy arrives at the hotel reception.

She speaks to the porter.

-Is Phil Lynott staying here?

-Sorry, I cannot help you.

Lizzy bungs him a twenty-pound note.

-Yes, Room 24.

Lizzy smiles at the porter and heads for the lift.

Phil opens the door. Lizzy throws her arms around him.

-Lizzy it's great to see you. How did you find me?

I really missed you, this time round.

Lizzy sees the coke laid out in lines, on a glass table.

-Me too. You're not still taking the stuff, Phil?

-It's my business, Lizzy?

-It is my business Phil, I love you. I'm clean now Phil. I know what it's like, I was so screwed up. Look, Phil your ruining your life.

You've got a great career. You're going to kill yourself, you'll end up like Hendrix.

-You don't understand, Lizzy. I'm under a lot of pressure.

I've come so far, but I feel I've got nowhere, - You got to get a grip on yourself, Phil.

-Rock and roll, I thought would set me free. But I'm still screwed up and confused.

-Look, Phil you've achieved so much for rock in Ireland. You're an example to all those young Irish people out there.

-I've grown dependent on drugs. It makes me forget. I suppose things wouldn't have been any different. I'm

black and I'm white, I'm Irish and I'm not. I'm a poor Crumlin boy and a rock star. I lost myself somewhere.

-Get a grip on yourself Phil!

-America's the next stop.

-America! Slow down, Phil, what are you trying to prove?

-Maybe that some poor boy from Crumlin can make it big. I'm sorry, Lizzy, for throwing all this shit at you.

-It's okay, Phil. I'm trying to understand. I never had such problems. It seems to me that you've climbed a long way up, but now you are falling faster.

-I've got to crack America.

-If you don't give it up, I'm not going to see you anymore. Lizzy turns to leave.

-Don't go Lizzy, stay with me!

-If you really loved me, Phil, you'd give it up.

Lizzy walks out and gently closes the door behind her.

She walks out to the street and hails a taxi. Phil stands at the window, watching.

***

Phil takes a taxi ride through Dublin and looks out vacantly at the city. He gets out at the docks and walks down to the water-front. The sun is rising. Phil stops at the pier and sits down on a bench. Seagulls fly above him. Trawlers make their way out to sea. He starts humming to himself a new song her wrote. - Dear Lord, give me dignity, restore my sanity, my vanity is killing me.

***

The next day sees Phil walking down the street in Crumlin. He walks into his local grocer's to buy cigarettes. Inside are some old ladies in their curlers. Some of them recognise Phil.

-Jasus Phil, it's yourself!

-How's it going, Molly?

-I saw you on top of the Pops, you were really great. Phyllis must be proud of you.

-Phil, you're a star. I remember ya when you were only a nipper - a Crumlin lad. She slaps Phil on the back, laughing. Meanwhile word has

got out that Phil's back in Crumlin. Screams can be heard outside the door.

-What's that?

-I got to get outa here, more groupies. He exits the shop to see crazed women running

114

down the street. He ducks and nips down an alley and over a back fence. He runs back to his house.

Peter opens the front door.

-What's up, Phil?

-More groupies.

-Jasus, I wish they were running after me, most of the women I get look like the back of a bus. ***

Phil returns to his house, Timmy, Pete and Gran are there to meet them at the door.

-Great to see you all.

-How's it going Phil?

-Great, the band's doing great.

-I sometimes wish he'd try something else. That nephew of yours has lost so much weight.

Well, I'm going to fatten him up while he is here.

Pete opens a bottle of whiskey.

-Well, let's drink to our grand re-union.

They toast each other.

***

The next day Phil attends a gig in Moran's Hotel.

The Boomtown Rats are performing. Bob Geldof nods to Phil. Projected images of giant rats appear behind the band as well as pictures of rats in space. Bob lets rip across the audience.

-Who were the first in space? Who are the greatest enemies of mankind! Rats!

Bob opens a cage and throws a white live rat into the crowd. The girls scream in terror.

-Everyone, do the Rat!

Geldof takes a raw fish from the fly of his jeans. It looks totally phallic. A poster of the wall reads.

GELDOF IS GOD.

***

Later that night Phil is in the hall of the Moran's Hotel, watching Bob Geldof, who is stage.

-D'ya wanna change the world?

Yeah.

You can change the world-your world and everybody else's world We got to get off our arses and build a better life here in Ireland. Screw the politicians who sit on the fence. We need action, music can change the world. Our world! The audience applaud and Geldof breaks into the song Banana Republic.

Banana Republic

Pigs and priests,

Geldof sings Rat Trap.

Just down past the gasworks, by the meat factory door

It's a rat trap, Billy, but you're already caught.

Phil meets up with Bob backstage later.

-Jasus Bob that was a great gig, great stuff. Love the Lyrics, angry stuff.

-I am an angry young man; it's a Banana republic full of pigs and priests!

-I am going to give up the day job and concentrate on the band.

-What day job. Asked Phil.

-I'm working on an abattoir.

An abattoir what that. Said Phil.

It's a place you kill animals, sheep, cows, whatever needs killing.

-Jasus that's tough work Bob.

-You can say that again I am on the night shift, the graveyard shift.

-Have you recorded a demo yet Bob?

-Look Ill give you the address, if you drop around tomorrow I'll give a demo. - You mean the abattoir. Said Phil.

-Yeah I'll give you a demo of how to kill a cow in five seconds.

-Bono, arrives, with his band The Hype.

-Jasus The Hype is here. Said Geldof.

-This is Bono.

-Hi Phil, I've been to see your gigs many times.

This is Larry, Adam and the Edge.

-Hallow boys, join us and have a beer.

-That was a great gig Bob.

-Its angry stuff, but I have no time for the hypocrisy in Ireland. I am heading over to England.

-I have some good contacts for you in the record business. Said Phil.

We are looking for a record deal too. Said Bono.

-Don't worry, I have loads of contacts.

Bill Graham from Hot Press shows up. The other Rats members arrive behind him. Simon Crowe, Pete Briquette and Garry Roberts along with B. P Fallon - Bill great to see you.

-Great gig Bob. I'll get you the front page of Hot Press.

-You're goona be big, just hang in there.

-B.P how's it going. Said Phil.

-Great, Phil Ive got the NME magazine front page for you too Phil.

-Cool you can handle all my publicity. Where did you get that suit? It looks like a bleedin pyjamas.

-I am not a civil servant; I am a rock promoter.

-Nice One B.P you have style.

***

Outside Morans Pub, high heels can be heard clanking along the street an old lady sees two transsexuals approaching her.

-You ought to be ashamed of yourself, dressed like that.

-Are you men or women?

No missus, we're transsexuals.

***

They hurry inside. Bono greets Pod and Gucci.

- This is Pod and Gucci. The have a band called the Virgin Prunes.

A tall handsome boy in a suit walks in. Bono turns to him.

-Gavin great to see you. Meet Gavin Friday he's in the Prunes too.

-Good to meet you, have a beer. Said Phil pointing to the beer cans.

-Were talking about record deals. Said Bono.

-You got to come up with a new name Bono. Said

Phil.

-Why is that Phil?

-It's a bit obvious and a bit cheap. The Hype sounds like a name for an old folks dance band.

-Bono has come up with a new name for the band. Said Gavin.

-I told him the Hype, was crap, but he would not listen to me. What have you come up with?

-U2. Said Bono, looking at Gavin intensely.

What's that supposed to mean U2! It sound like a sales pitch for selling washing powder, like Daz! Said Phil.

-No Phil, U2 is the name of an American spy plane. We are in the cold war. It a political name. It more hardcore, political Gavin. Can't you see that.

I was watching a movie about the American pilot Gary Powers the other night. His spy plane was shot down over Russia. The plane was called U2. Said Bono convincingly.

-Now that sounds more like it! Said Phil.

-Well you're the main man Phil. I'll take your advice. U2 it is.

-Ok, it took us ages to come up with the Virgin Prunes. Said Gavin.

-You don't look like virgins to me, but a bunch of trannies. Said Phil swigging on his beer.

-He's right Bono, come up with something more interesting like your name Bono. Where did you pick that up? Said Larry.

-It's a hearing aid shop in Mary st, called Bono Vox. Guggi and Gavin Friday in the Virgin Prunes, came up with it.

-Do the Prunes need a record deal. Said Phil.

We have a record deal, with Rough Trade Records.

They it's called "Twenty Tens, 'I've Been Smoking All Night'

-Could you not come up with something more original. Hearing aids and smoking, sounds crap to me. Said Phil.

-No, no its, we laid down some good tracks.

We have a great line up. With Gavin Friday and Guggi, along with a third vocalist; Dave-iD Busaras, guitarist Dik Evans, The Edge.

-Id Busaras, you have called your guitarist after a bus station. Are you sure what you're up to Gavin? Said Phil. Maybe Phils right, the Virgin Prunes is a bit crap; names about smoking, buses and hearing aids does not sound very original to me; and now spy planes. Said Gavin looking worried.

-How about Celtic Messiah. The Committed, The Dole Busters. Said Guggi.

-Naw sounds crap. Think outside the box! Said Phil. - I will give it some thought.

We're having a gig in the Dandelion Market next week. At the top of Grafton St. You are both invited. It only fifty pence to get in but you can come for free.

Said Bono. What's your real name. Said Phil.

-Paul !

How about St Paul and the Messiah's. Said Phil with a wide grin on his face.

-I had the same problem with my band. Said Bob.

The original name was 'The Nightlife Thugs, but when Garry threatened to resign, if we were called that. So I came up with the "Boomtown Rats" after a gang of children that I read about in Woody Guthrie's autobiography, Bound for Glory - Your bound for glory Phil!

-Maybe we all are. Who knows. We are all in the gutter but some of us are looking at the stars.

-Look boys I will give you some intros to record companies. Maybe you can support me. I've been offered a gig at Slane Castle. Bono how about it. It will hold thousands. I'ts run by an English toff called Henry Mount Charles. I can get you a gig there too.

-Fantastic Bob, you're a star. Without you Phil, the Irish rock scene would be going nowhere.

-Someone has to be the leader of the pack boys. You will lead the pack someday too

Bono and Bob. You just got to hang on in there. Phil looked up. In walked a tall handsome man with long flowing hair. With a curly haired man with curly hair carrying a guitar.

-Loved you gig. Said the man in an American accent.

Your American. Said Phil.

-Yeah, The name Scott, Scott Gorham. I loved you gig Bob it was cool.

-Thanks.

Scott turned to his curly haired friend.

-This is Brian Roberson, he's a Scotsman.

-Ach aye I'm from Glasgow. I heard that Dublin was a happening scene, so I took the boat as soon as I could.

-Well you came to the right place.

-Were looking to join a band. Said Scott.

-What do you play.

-Electric guitar.

-Cool, you can join my band if your any good. The Rats and the Hyper are top heavy.

-What's the band called?

-Thin Lizzy!

-Cool. I'm going to write a song about all us boys. I'm going to call it 'The Boys Are Back in Town'.

-Right on, Philo. Said Bono.

-It will be an anthem to all our struggles!

***

The next day Phil grabs a taxi to Bob abattoir in Ballsbridge. He enters the half open door and finds Bob wearing a long apron, covered in blood. In his hand he holds a gun. Around him lies carcasses of cows with bullets between their eyes.

-Jasus Bob, you look like a serial killer. A you man walks by.

-This is Billy my assistant. Meet Phil Irelands greatest rock star.

-Hi'ya Billy. Said Phil, realising that he is standing in a pool of blood.

-Come inside. Said Bob looking at his pointed cowboy boots.

Billy put on the tea.

-So you see why I want to become a rock star and get out of this place. Said Bob.

-Here's the demo. Rat Trap is on this tape and Banana Republic.

-I like the title said Phil.

-It is a Banana Republic. This country is run by pigs and priests. The Catholic Church has a lot to answer for.

-I'm packing in this job next week. The records are beginning to sell.

-It 'aint a life shooting cattle.

It's easy, you wait several minutes, until one of the cattle is standing in just the right position. The bullet needs to hit a certain, spot on the forehead so that the animal is stunned instantly. This isn't something just any amateur can do.

-You don't belong here Bob pack it in. I'll see if I can get you a record deal.

-Thanks Phil, you're a star.

As the boys have some tea. Bono calls around.

-Bono, what are you doing here.

-I brought a demo tape over.

-Sit down, Billy will get you a cup of tea.

-Jasus Bob, you have a rough job. Said Bono eyeing the hanging carcasses dripping in blood.

-It pays the bills, I have my father and sister to look after.

-Where is your mother?

-I am close to death here Phil. It reminds me of my mother's death. She died of a brain haemorrhage.

-Jesus, the same thing happened to my mother!

-Sorry to hear that Bono.

-She died when I was fourteen, I miss her.

-Do you remember her Bob?

I remember little things, they come back to me, like flashes in my mind. Her velvet glove on her right hand, lipstick on a china tea cup, I remember running my little finger through her hair, while sitting on her knee. I feel a sense of loss, rooted down deep inside me.

That's where the pain comes from, a sort of feeling of emptiness,

-I feel the same way Bob, sometimes. My mother died too when I was young. We have been through the same pain, the same loss. Said Bono.

-I was fourteen. It was in 1974. The 10 September. It was a cold winters day. It was the day my father was buried at Glasnevin cemetery. She had a cerebral aneurysm. Maybe she loved him so much that the death of her great love was too much for her to bear.

I wrote a song about it.

"I Will Follow'.

-I remember the pain I felt when I was fifteen, when I would come home to an empty house in Dun Laoghaire. My father, was a traveling salesman. He was always away all week. I had two older sisters, but they were not living there anymore.

-I had that sense a bizarre fear of coming home. The house is dark, I walked up the steps and I would open the door. I would keep my head down. I felt that if I did not keep my head down at the top of the stairs, my mother looking at me.

Did you think here spirit; her ghost was still in the house. Said Bono.

-Maybe, her spirit was certainly there. I loved her. It was not the time for her to go. She was taken away, for no reason.

-I remember the night before she died. The fading evening light penetrated through the window. I was sitting in the bay window with my mother and a friend. I decided to go to bed and had a quick cuddle with her. I was sharing a bedroom with my sister. Her friend Olivia was over and they were going to have a midnight feast.

I asked them to wake me so I could join in. I did wake up in the middle of the night, but they told me to go back to sleep as it wasn't midnight yet. I said: 'I can hear you crying.' But they said 'No, we're laughing', so I went back to sleep.

-When I woke up the next morning, it was quiet. Then my father came up and very bluntly told me, that my mother died that night. He started crying, and I started crying. Her death came out of the blue, you know, there was no warning or lingering illness. Just bang, she was gone.

-Afterwards I was packed off to stay with some relatives, as in those days' children didn't go to funerals. I remember going back to school and the boys kept a distance, and the priests, who were being over kind.

-It was unbearable to be that small and to have to take care of yourself. At the time, I just get on with it and it becomes routine to shop, to cook and to get the coal from the basement to light the fire. - Sorry boys, I lost myself. Said Bob sadly.

***

Phil heads back on the Crumlin Road. He passes the dole office. There's a queue a mile long stretching down the street. Phil spots Macker coming out.

-Phil how's the buzz, man?

-How's G.I. Joe?

-Well, Philo, the Joy is not the bleeding Ritz. It's just three meals a day and a bed. If you could call them meals, the food's crap.

-I'm going to sort him out next week.

-Come on, Phil, Let's go for a beer. Some of the boys are around.

Phil follows Macker into a bar and bumps straight into Brush.

-Phil! It's good to see you!

Big Lee walks out of the gents.

-Well if it isn't Philo himself! What's it like being a bleedin rock star?

-Tough!

-You probably has loads of women and drinking champagne.

-You can get bored of that too!

-Well, you got off the dole queue Philo and that's a bleedin achievement in Ireland.

-We must party together sometime. Like the old days.

Anytime, Philo. Drop down to the Baggot.

Phil turns to the barman.

-Free beers for everyone.

***

Phil holes up in the Clarence hotel. Papers are scattered across the table. He writes the lyrics for

'The Boys Are Back in Town'

Guess who just back today?

Those wild eyed boys had been away.

***

A few weeks later the Thin Lizzy van speeds down country lanes. They pull up outside a giant ballroom with the name "Palace" written in neon lights. A lone saxophone player plays outside. Phil struts up, with his guitar.

-Is Big Al around?

-He's in the office.

Phil walks into the office. Big Al is sitting there, counting a pile of money.

-You must be Phil Lynott, there's not that many black Irishman round here.

-That's right.

-You're on tonight.

-What kind of crowd do you get round here?
- It's empty now, but every farmer from miles around will be here soon. You're sharing the bill with Roy Orbison.

-Looks like you're making money.

-Well, I've got twenty ballrooms but I have one great ambition.

-What's that?

-To be Prime Minister of Ireland.

***

Further away, a Cadillac is speeding across a field towards the ballroom. Inside sits Roy Orbison, with a man in a Texan hat at the wheel. The car grinds to a halt and gets stuck in the mud.

-Damn roads.

-Let's walk, they never told me the roads were so bad over here. Roy struts up to the door of the ballroom where the sax player guides him towards the office. Big Al greets him.

-Well, if it ain't the man himself.

-It's been a long hike from Dublin.

***

That night Phil crashes in a local hotel. Hundreds of groupies stand screaming outside. Phil pulls back the curtains.

-What the is going on? Said Brian.

-They're groupies, a new breed of women. A groupie wants sex with a hero, a star, a big shot like you, Phil.

They want to attain nirvana in your arms, the rock star is the high priest of western civilisation.

***

The next day Phil goes downstairs and tries to leave the hotel. The police are holding the crowd back. The girls scream hysterically.

-Oh, Phil, we love ya, Phil. Screams one girl.

Phil dives into the van with the band. It takes off down the street, followed by hundreds of groupies. ***

Weeks later Phil and the band are performing their new single- "The Boys are Back in Town." It's the National Ballroom, 1976 and hundreds of people stand listening.

***

Back in Dublin Radio the Larry Gogan show is at its peak. Gogan's playing "The Boys Are Back in

Town."

***

Thin Lizzy have hit the big time with: 'The Boys Are Back in Town, topping the charts around the world. This major success of an Irish rock band, has sparked off the music scene in Dublin. Hundreds of fans are jamming, following in the footsteps of Phil Lynott.

***

Back in Crumlin, Peter and Phil's Gran sit watching TV.

-Listen to this! Phil's done it!

Peter turns up the radio. "The Boys Are Back in Town"soars around the room.

-He's reached the top ten in Britain and America, He's done it! He's made it. Well, Phil is an example to us all, so long as it doesn't blow his mind.

-Does that mean he's rich?

Gran watches with mouth open in disbelief. Tears roll down her cheeks.

-He's done it. He'll never have to work again.

-I don't believe it, Phil's our boy.

-It's Acapulco for me.

-Well, it's Mullen's bar for a pint for me. So, Phil finally beat the dole queues of Crumlin!
***

Phil listens to Larry Gogan's Radio show.

-The Boomtown Rats have moved to London. Signing a recording contract with Ensign Records, they released their debut single, "Lookin' After No. 1". Their debut album, The Boomtown Rats, was released, in the UK and on Mercury Records in the United States.

The Rats signed a recording contract with Ensign

Records, they released their debut single, 'Lookin' After No. 1'. Their debut album, The Boomtown Rats, was released on Ensign in the UK and on Mercury Records in the United States, and featured another "Geldof's moody charisma helped to give the band a distinct identity". The Rats are headed this month on an American tour.

Geldof, is releasing a new song, after reading a telex report at Georgia State University's campus radio station, WRAS, on the shooting spree of sixteenyear-old; Brenda Ann Spencer, who fired at children in a school playground, killing two adults and injuring eight children and one police officer. Spencer showed no remorse for her crime and her full explanation for her actions was "I don't like Mondays. This livens up the day". The song was first performed, less than a month later. Geldof explained how he wrote the song:

-Geldorf said; I was doing a radio interview in Atlanta with Johnny Fingers and there was a telex machine beside me. I read it as it came out. Not liking Mondays as a reason for shooting somebody, was a bit strange. I was thinking about it on the way back to the hotel and I just said 'Silicon chip inside her head had switched to overload'. I wrote that down. And the journalists interviewing her said, 'Tell me why?' It was such a senseless act. 'Her reply was I don't like Mondays'. The song is now UK number one single.

***

Lizzy meets Phil at the Clarence Hotel, waiting for Phil.

-Phil, congratulations! You've done it!

-It's been a long time coming.

The chauffeur arrives.

-The limmo's ready, to take you to the airport.

-Ok, Gus, I'll be there soon.

-Where are you off to?

-America.

-America!

-Yes - do you want to come?

-Are you serious?

-Course I'm serious.

Lizzy throws her arms around him and kisses him - Oh, I'd love to!

***

They get ready and both climb into the limmo. Phil speaks to the chauffeur.

139

-There's just something I have to do, let's go to Crumlin.

***

They cruise along the streets of Crumlin, to Phil's old home. His family are waiting for him; his Ma, Gran, Tim and Pete.

-Ma! You made it!

-Phil! We're so proud of you!

-This is Lizzy, Gran, uncle Pete and uncle Tim.

-Lovely to meet you.

-I'm going to America!

Children gather outside the house, cheering.

-How are ya Phil? You're looking bleeding great. Said Pete.

-I've got to catch a flight, I'm late, Gran.

-Can you drop me off at the factory. I am work in Guinness Brewery now.

-Well, I'll drop you off too.

They all climb in and wave goodbye to Pete.

***

The limmo arrives at the factory. Workers stands outside, cheering.

-Phil you've done well, best of luck. Said Tim.

-Good luck Philo, I'll be thinking of you.

-Me too.

***

Phils limo cruises along towards Dublin airport.

-Who would ever have thought that we would ever be in the back of a limmo!

-To be sure, it's a long way from Crumlin!

As they pass through the Dublin streets, people stop to stare at them and waive at Phil. Robbo and Scott are waiting outside the Gresham Hotel with their gear. The jump in the limo.

***

Two hours later the plane carrying them all takes off.

Phil and Lizzy hours later sees the Statue of Liberty appearing on the horizon.

***

Ten years later

Lizzy Diary;

11 th January 1984.

I heard of his death on the radio. I could not believe it. At Howth Parish Church a crowd of mourners gathered for the funeral of Ireland's greatest rock star Phil Lynott. Bono, Bob Geldof, Paula Yates and Charles Haughey, the Irish Prime Minister attended the funeral. They sang the hymn

'Praise my Soul, the King of Heaven.'

On his coffin were the words; PHILIP PARIS LYNOTT .

May God give peace to his soul Lizzy.

He was the uncrowned King of Irish rock. I went to the St Finians Cemetery I lay a red rose after everyone had left. The headstone had the inscription

***

Back in Crumlin, Uncle Pete listens to the radio. - Today the wild man of Irish rock,

Philip Lynott was buried in a cemetery on a hill in Howth overlooking

Dublin. Lynott was Ireland's first rock star, that inspired bands like U2 and The Boom Town Rats.

Lynott was a true rock and roller, blazing a trail across the world for sixteen years before his candle burned out with the excesses of drugs and his rock and roll lifestyle. His music influenced such bands as Bon Jovi and Gun and Roses. Today he is a folk hero in the world of music and Ireland. His tragic death at thirty-six is a loss not only to Ireland but to the world of music.

***

U2 went on to become the world's greatest rock band, selling millions of records. Bono has become one of the world's best-known charitable performers and was named the most politically effective celebrity of all time. Bono has become increasingly involved in campaigning for third world debt relief and raising awareness of the plight of Africa. In Ireland he is regarded as the greatest 'missionary' to leave our shores since Edel

Quinn who died trying to save the poor of Africa.

In 1984 Bob and Midge Ure founded the charity super group Band Aid to raise money for famine relief in Ethiopia. They went on to organize the charity super concert Live Aid. The following year and the Live 8 concerts in 2005. Bob Geldof raised eighty million pounds for the starving people of Ethiopia.

***

Bob has been nominated for the Nobel Peace Prize, was granted an honorary knighthood by Queen

Elizabeth II, and given the title Sir Bob.

In 2009 the parole board ruled that Brenda Ann

Spencer the woman that inspired Bob song 'I don't Like Mondays', would be denied parole, and would not be considered for the next ten years. She will become eligible to have a Board of Parole Hearing in 2019.

Roy Orbinson went back to America and never returned. GI Joe was last seen at Dublin airport taking a flight to Jamaica.

As for Macker, well he's running a rag and bone shop off Camden street. He's still got Phil's guitar hanging inside the front door. The Dice man succumbed to some terrible illness and died. We carried his coffin down Grafton street as a mark of a deep respect. As for Mad Mick Mulcahy, he escaped from Dublin and we heard that he had found 'love' with a country maiden. Louis Walsh did make it big with Johnny Logan, who won the Eurovision song Contest.

Guggi is now a world famous painter. Gavin Friday is still close friends of Bono and producing records. On rare occasions Bono and the Edge is spotted in Grafton street. Some say that he moved out to the sea coats of Killiney and bough a big pad. Others believe that he's in Manhattan or Monte Carlo. We are all certain that where ever he is, he's still trying to save the world. Some people think he should be canonised as a saint or even nominated to be Pope.

Philomena Lynott still lives in Howth and appear from time to time at the 'Vibe for Phil', gigs organised by Brush Shields and his buddy's. Phil's father has not been heard from in a long time. Some believe he returned to his roots in South America,

As for Thin Lizzy she still lives in Dublin. Every year on Philips anniversary, she places a red rose on his grave. Sometimes people see this lone figure of Lizzy, with her Pre-Raphaelite features and long flowing hair to her waist, standing at Phil's grave. But they are too far away to see tears streaming down her face. She keeps all her love letters under lock and key, in a box under her bed. In it lies many more untold secrets of how Irish rock scene started. She tells her friends, from time to time these stories - but no one believes her, but I do; the truth is always stranger than fiction.

***

Notes and Music Credits

Song lyrics are as cited within fair use - De Minimis

United States, the Copyright Act 1976 (Title 17 of the United States Code, controls fair use. Section 107, 106, 106A.)

UK. Copyright, Designs and Patents Act 1988 (the 1988 Act),

Notes; Music credits;

Hot press Article excerpt;11 March 2011.

Remembering Philo.

Hot Press – 4 June 2009 – My mother Death – Julia Ogivly.

Independent.ie - 14 April – 2013

The Saving of Geldof's Soul – by Barry Egan.

Roddy Doyle –The Commitments. Quote.

Barbara Mikkelson (29 September 2005). "Urban Legends Reference Pages: Music (I Don't Like Mondays)".

Clarke, Steve (1979) "The Fastest Lip on Vinyl", Smash Hits, EMAP National Publications Ltd, 18–31 October 1979, p.6-7.

Lyrics quotes.

I remember that summer in Dublin.

Songwriter: LIAM REILLY

Little Black Boy.

Phil Lynott.

Black Boys On The Corner lyrics © Universal Music Publishing Group

Don't Believe a Word.

©Philip Parris Lynott.

New Day.

©Philip Parris Lynott.

Whiskey in the Jar.

© Unknown.

Got to Give It Up.

©Philip Parris Lynott.

Banana Republic.

©Bob Geldof. Pete Briquette.

Rat Trap.

©Bob Geldof. Pete Briquette.

The Boys are Back in Town.

©Philip Parris Lynott.

Photos

Brain Downey, Phil Lynott, Eric Bell,
Thin Lizzy

Brain Robertson, Phil Lynott,

Scott, Gorham, Brain Downey

Brian Robertson, Brain Downey,

Phil Lynott, Scott Gorham

U2

Manager Pau; Mc Guinness and U2.

The man himself – Bobo.

Bob Geldof– rock star, saver of millions,
inspiration to all - knighted.

Boomtown Rats

Bill Graham (1951 – 11 May 1996) was an Irish journalist and author. He attended Blackrock College and Trinity College, Dublin and resided in Howth. In addition to authoring several books, Graham wrote for Hot Press magazine from its founding. He died of a heart attack at forty-four on 11 May 1996 being survived by his mother Eileen.

Graham's long-time colleague and Hot Press editor Niall Stokes described him:

"In many ways, he was a founding father of modern Irish music. He inspired a whole generation of Irish fans and musicians to look at the world in a different and broader light. And he was good on more than music too. He felt a kinship with Northern Ireland and the people on both sides of the sectarian and political divide there that was unusual in those who were brought up within the narrow confines of the culture of Ireland in the '60s and '70s – and his political writing reflected this. And he was also ahead of the game in terms of his appreciation of the importance of the politics of food and the position of the developing world in the new era."

Graham was instrumental in the formation of Irish rock band U2, having brought them to the attention of their manager Paul McGuinness. At a recent exhibition of early group photos, McGuinness remembered the role Bill Graham played by introducing him to the band. Despite being widely known as the man who "discovered" U2, it was a title he disavowed. He wrote enthusiastically about the band, giving them their first exposure. Both guitarist The Edge and Bono have explained Graham's role in the band's development.

John Waters observed that "It is often said that Bill 'discovered' U2. This is untrue. Bill created U2, through his enthusiasm for them. He gave them a reflection of their own possibilities and they only looked back that once"... He had a "deep knowledge of virtually every form of popular and roots music... and Waters goes on to credit him as 'the first Irish writer to write about the connection between Irish political culture and Irish rock'n'roll'.

Books

Book written by Graham include Enya: The Latest Score, U2: In the name of love: a history and Complete Guide to the Music of U2.

Influence

A number of music critics/journalists have cited Graham as a primary influence, in some cases suggesting they got into the field as a direct result of his writing, e.g. Jim Carroll, Irish Times, June 2012–

"I blame it all on Bill Graham, the brilliant Hot Press writer who sadly waltzed off this mortal coil in 1996. I blame dear old Bill for lots of things. I'll be honest: without him, I probably would never have been a music writer in the first place and you wouldn't be reading this. I used to say that to wind him up when we'd meet and he'd groan aloud. I mean, there are a lot of things to carry the rap for and the shit I've written over the years is a damn heavy burden to bear.... Bill's feature took my breath away. Here was someone writing with an unsurpassed degree of passion, fervour, belief, enthusiasm, knowledge and depth about one of my favourite bands. I must have read that piece about a hundred times. I had already heard the big music, but now I'd seen the big picture. I had found my career. And I had found the fever."

His funeral drew many of biggest bands from the world of Irish music including Clannad, Altan, U2 and Hothouse Flowers, along with singers Simon Carmody and Gavin Friday.

Shay Healy (29 March 1943 – 9 April 2021) was an Irish songwriter, broadcaster and journalist. He is best known for his role as host of Nighthawks, a RTÉ Television chat show of the late 1980s and early 1990s, and for composing "What's Another Year", Ireland's winning entry in the 1980 Eurovision Song Contest.

Early life

Shay Healy was raised along with his five siblings in Sandymount in Dublin. His father, Seamus, was a civil servant and part-time stage actor who performed at the Abbey and Olympia theatres. His mother, Máirín Ní Shúilleabháin, was a singer of Irish traditional songs. She also wrote plays and stories and encouraged young Shay's early talent for writing. This led to his first appearance at the age of 15 on the Irish national radio station, Radió Éireann, reading a self-penned article.

Career

Healy had a varied career, never focusing too intently on any one of his various professional interests. Of his tendency to diversify he once commented: "I know it infuriates some people when you don't pigeonhole yourself, but I don't take on anything that won't stand up to public scrutiny."

Songwriting

Healy first received attention as a performer of his own "songs of social significance" during the 1960s. Later he wrote comedy songs for Billy Connolly, including "The Orient Express-a tale of intrigue and cross dressing", "The Shitkickers Waltz", and "The Country & Western Supersong". Healy achieved his greatest success as a songwriter with "What's Another Year", which won the 1980 Eurovision Song Contest. Over the course of the next 15 years, the song earned him a total of £250,000. In 1983 his song, "Edge Of

The Universe", sung by Linda Martin, was the overall winner of the Castlebar Song Contest. Under the name of Crack, he and Dave
Pennefather released a parody song called "Silly Fellow", which was about Paul McCartney's arrest and jail experience in Japan. unreliable source?]
Healy and Pennefather also released a parody of Abba's song "Mamma Mia" that they called "Hey C'mere" and credited to Rubbish.

Musical theatre

In 1977, Healy branched into musical theatre with the script, co-written with Niall Toibin, for a stage production entitled The King. This was a show based on the life and music of Elvis Presley and was premiered at the Cork Opera House two months after the singer's death. In contrast, Healy's rock opera, The Knowledge, failed to receive commercial backing and was premiered in Dundalk by an amateur group in January 1989.

Healy was more successful with his musical, The Wiremen, which received its premiere on 4 May 2005 at Dublin's Gaiety

Theatre in a production by John McColgan and Moya Doherty that ran for six weeks. The Wiremen tells the story of the introduction of electricity into County Mayo during the 1950s. In March 2010 the show was revived in an amateur production by the Birr Stage Guild.

Broadcasting

Healy joined RTÉ Television in 1963 as a trainee cameraman. Within five years he had moved to the other side of the lens with appearances on programmes such as Twenty Minutes With., Ballad Sheet and Hoot'nany.

In the summer months of 1988 he hosted a series called The Dublin Village with Ingrid Miley it reran on Wednesday nights in 2005 and 2006 on RTE 2.

Between 1988 and 1992 Healy hosted Nighthawks, a late-night satirical chat show broadcast on RTÉ Two, which he later described as "the best four years of my working life". In January 1992, the show became embroiled in political controversy as a result of Healy's interview with former Fianna Fáil Justice Minister Seán Doherty. During the interview, Doherty revealed that some members of the cabinet with whom he served in 1982 had been aware of his order to illegally tap the phones of a number of Irish journalists. The revelation led to the resignation of Taoiseach Charles Haughey a few weeks later.

In January 1995, RTÉ terminated Healy's contract.

One of his last shows for the station was Where Are They Now? in which he interviewed former celebrities whose fame had largely faded. Healy then set up his own production company which made a series of television documentaries. His 1995 TV documentary on Irish musician, Phil Lynott, The Rocker, was broadcast on RTÉ Two and BBC Two, and later released as a DVD. In 1998, Healy made two half-hour documentaries for the RTÉ One television series, Against The Odds. The series focused on individuals who had overcome adversity in their lives. Healy's two films featured an actor, Chris Burke, who was born with dwarfism, and a singer, Ronan Tynan, whose legs were amputated when he was twenty.

Among the other TV programmes Healy presented were Reach For The Stars (1971), Hullaballoo (1977), The Birthday Show (1993-1995), Beastly Behaviour (1998-1999), Ireland's Greatest Hits (2001) and A Little Bit Country (2006).

Healy won two Jacob's Awards. He received the first in 1984 for Strawberry Fields Forever, a radio documentary series on the 1960s in Ireland, which he presented and Siobhan McHugh produced. His second award came in 1989 for his television work. In 2007, Healy joined the judging panel on TG4's talent show, Glór Tíre.

Writing

In the early 1960s, Healy became Folk Correspondent for Spotlight, an Irish pop music weekly, and he continued to write for the magazine until its demise in the mid-1970s. He wrote a weekly column for the Irish Daily Mail.

The Stunt is the title of Healy's debut novel, published in 1992. It deals with the Irish rock scene and was described by one reviewer as "a more truthful... representation (of) the Irish music scene than The

Commitments". His second novel, Green Card Blues, is set among the illegal Irish immigrant community in New York City.

In 2005 On The Road, Healy's memoir of his life in show business, was published.

In 2004, Healy was diagnosed with the degenerative disorder, Parkinson's disease. Healy died on 9 April 2021, aged 78.

Publications

The Stunt, (O'Brien Press, 1992, ISBN 978-0-86278322-8)

Green Card Blues, (O'Brien Press, 1994, ISBN 9780-86278-386-0)

Beastly Jokes, (O'Brien Press, 2005, ISBN 978-086278-923-7)

More Beastly Jokes, (O'Brien Press, 2005, ISBN 978-0-86278-924-4)

On The Road, (O'Brien Press, 2005, ISBN 978-086278-949-7)

Thomas McGinty (1 April 1952 – 20 February 1995), known as The Diceman, was a Scottish-Irish actor, model, and street artist specialising in mime. Born in Scotland of Irish parentage, McGinty spent much of his life and career in Ireland, where he became a landmark living statue and one of the country's most popular street performers. He appeared in various plays and films, and through his work promoted political causes including gay rights in Ireland; he has been dubbed a "gay icon". He died in 1995 at age 42, from complications of AIDS.

Life and career

Thomas McGinty was born in the outskirts of Glasgow on 1 April 1952, to Thomas and Mary McGinty (née O'Hara), both of whom had previously lived in Ireland. At least one of Thom's parents were of Irish origin – Mary was born in Baltinglass, County Wicklow – which granted him Irish citizenship. He had two sisters; the family would holiday each summer in Mary's hometown.

McGinty served as an altar boy and considered becoming a priest. Instead, he studied accountancy at Strathclyde University, but dropped out. He was a member of Strathclyde Theatre Group in the early 1970s before moving to Ireland in 1976 to work as a nude model at the National College of Art and Design. The name "The Diceman" came from one of McGinty's employers, The Diceman Games Shop that was located, first, in an arcade on Grafton Street, Dublin, and then on South Anne Street.

McGinty specialised in standing in the street, stock still and in complete silence, and in costume, for long periods of time like a living statue, and would disturb his immobility only to perform his trademark broad, saucy, pantomime wink to reward anyone who put money at his feet. When the Gardaí told him to move along for causing an obstruction in the street when crowds gathered to watch him, McGinty developed an extremely slow-motion walk that was really immobility in motion. Most of his costumes were exuberant and fanciful, and he appeared in such guises as the framed Mona Lisa, or Dracula, or as a light bulb, teapot, or clown. He was charged with breach of the peace and with wearing a costume which could offend public decency, on 15 June 1991, for a street performance in which he wore nothing but a skimpy loin cloth that failed to cover his buttocks.

McGinty called himself a "stillness artist" and "a human statue".

His first public performances in Dublin were as the "Dandelion Clown" at the Dandelion Market, a former bohemian market on St. Stephen's Green.[11] During the 1980s and early 1990s, he became wellknown and popular for performances on Grafton Street where he worked as a mime artist or otherwise performed in costume, to advertise the Diceman shop.[8] When that went out of business, he was hired to advertise various other establishments, including Bewley's café, and he also promoted political causes through his work such as gay rights, the Birmingham Six, and human rights in Tibet. He lived for a time in the early 1980s in Baile Éamon behind Spiddal in County Galway where he formed The Dandelion Theatre Company.

In 1989, he appeared in the Gate Theatre production of Oscar Wilde's Salome, directed by Steven Berkoff, which transferred to the Edinburgh Festival and then to South Carolina. Mc Ginty performed in The Maids by Jean Genet, and worked also in France, Holland, Germany, Russia, Spain, and Switzerland. He acted in two films, The Metal Man (1989) and Corkscrew (1990). He was a guest, twice, on the television chat programme, The Late Late Show, in the mid-1980s and again in 1994.

McGinty, who was of Scottish-Irish nationality, was considered an honorary Dubliner despite his Glasgow accent and origins. Hot Press dubbed him "Ireland's most famous street performer and an integral part of Grafton Street life for well over a decade". The Irish Independent labelled McGinty a "Dublin institution", as well as a "gay icon"–a viewpoint echoed by The Irish Times.

Death and tributes

McGinty was diagnosed with HIV in 1990. At Halloween 1994, a tribute and benefit event was held in his honour at the Olympia Theatre at which he was crowned High King of Ireland, and money was raised to buy medicines, and to pay for his funeral. Two weeks later, he openly discussed his struggle with AIDS on The Late Late Show, considered by TheJournal.ie to have been "a brave move at a time when few people were prepared to admit in public that they had caught the AIDS virus".

McGinty died on 20 February 1995 after a sudden decline, aged 42. His coffin was carried the length of Grafton Street by his friends past a large crowd, and was accompanied by long and sustained applause. In 1997, the Lord Mayor of Dublin, Brendan Lynch, renamed a corner of Meeting House Square in Temple Bar as

"The Diceman's Corner", where a plaque commemorates him. There was a tribute to McGinty in May 2001 when an exhibition of twenty of his most creative and colourful costumes, made mostly by Aidan Bradley and Kathy Kavanagh/Showtime.ie, was held during a music festival in Dublin Castle. Two poems about McGinty appeared in 2002: one called "Diceman" by Liam O'Meara, and the title poem of Paula Meehan's collection, "Dharmakaya", is also about him.

Become a still pool,

In the anarchic flow, the street's

Unceasing carnival

Of haunted and redeemed.

—Paula Meehan, Dharmakaya, for Thom McGinty.

The poet Brendan Kennelly wrote a tribute to McGinty in the course of which he said,

"Thom McGinty's magic has to do with his ability to mesmerise his audience, to lure them out of their busy city selves and to take them away into that land of perfect stillness where marvellous dreams are as normal as Bewley's sticky buns."

Actor Alan Stanford proposed in 2005 that Grafton Street should have a statue of the performer. A song called "Diceman" was released by Rocky de Valera and the Gravediggers in 2007. A plaque in memory of McGinty was unveiled at the Baltinglass courthouse during the Baltinglass Street Festival on 27 August 2010. There is another plaque dedicated to him in Tralee, on the footpath in Denny Street at the corner of Castle Street where he performed during the Rose of Tralee.

Thom's coffin funeral procession Grafton
street

At a reception in the Gresham Hotel before the 1986 Irish premiere of the film Mona Lisa: Thom McGinty with Bob Hoskins, Neil Jordan and Vincent McCabe. Photograph: Paddy Whelan

Philomena Lynott (1930 -2019) Philomena Lynott was an Irish author and entrepreneur. She was the mother of Thin Lizzy frontman Phil Lynott, and her autobiography, My Boy, documents their relationship. She was the proprietor of the Clifton Grange Hotel in Manchester, which provided accommodation for a number of bands in the 1970s including Thin Lizzy.

Biography

Philomena Lynott was born on 22 October 1930 as the fourth of nine children to Frank and Sarah Lynott in Dublin, and grew up in the Crumlin district of the city. She left school aged 13 and worked in an elderly people's home.

In 1947 Lynott took advantage of a viable job market in England, that needed labour to rebuild damage caused by World War II, finding work as a nurse in Manchester. She began a relationship with Cecil Parris, which led to Philip's birth on 20 August 1949. She suffered prejudice because Philip was illegitimate and mixed race and decided it would be best for him to be raised by her parents in Dublin. Lynott had two other children that she put up for adoption. She remained close to her son throughout his life but because she only saw him sporadically felt they were more like sister and brother or friends instead of a typical mother and son relationship.

In 1964 Lynott began a relationship with Dennis Keeley and the couple took over management of the Clifton Grange Hotel in Whalley Range, Manchester. Though they had no experience in running a hotel, they bought the property after six months and remained there for the next 14 years. The hotel became well known in northwest England for being frequented by the show business trade. Lynott took advantage of hotel licensing laws, which meant the bar could be open at 2 am when all other local venues had shut. When Thin Lizzy became commercially successful in the 1970s, the band looked forward to gigging in Manchester as Philomena would accommodate them and put on an after-show party. Guitarist Brian Robertson recalls Philomena insisting on washing his hair before a television appearance, and later said she was "like everyone's mum, rolled into one." When the Sex Pistols played Manchester on the Anarchy Tour in December 1976, she was the only hotelier willing to accommodate them.

In 1980 Lynott and Keeley moved to Howth, County Dublin, into a house Philip bought for them. They later moved to Glen Corr, a house also in Howth. She was unaware of her son's history of drug abuse until late 1985. Lynott was not present at her son's bedside when he died on 4 January 1986 in Salisbury General Infirmary, having received a telephone call at her house in Kew that Philip was dead. Lynott suffered depression following her son's death and found it hard to come to terms with. She had a difficult relationship with her daughter-in-law, Caroline Crowther, after Philip's death and was forced to apply for a court order to see her grandchildren.

In the early 1990s, Lynott was approached by publishers asking if she would like to write her memoirs. She found the experience of re-examining the relationship with her son difficult, but rewarding. The book My Boy: The Philip Lynott Story was published by Hot Press Books in 1995. She regularly attended rock concerts around Dublin, and continued to commemorate Philip's life. She was a key figure in getting a bronze statue of him made and placed in Dublin in 2005, and was the special guest at Thin Lizzy fan events.

In 2012, Lynott objected to Mitt Romney's use of Thin Lizzy's "The Boys Are Back in Town" during his election campaign. In an interview with Irish rock magazine Hot Press, Philomena said, "As far as I am concerned, Mitt Romney's opposition to gay marriage and to civil unions for gays makes him antigay – which is not something that Philip would have supported."

Lynott died on 12 June 2019, after suffering from cancer for a number of years. The Irish President Michael D. Higgins praised her work campaigning for LGBT rights and against drug use.

Published works

Lynott, Philomena; Hayden, Jackie (1995). Niall Stokes (ed.). My Boy: The Philip Lynott Story. Hot Press Books. ISBN 978-0-753-50048-4.

Phil with his father Parris, from Guyana, South America, and Philomena his mother.

Phil childhood days Crumlin.

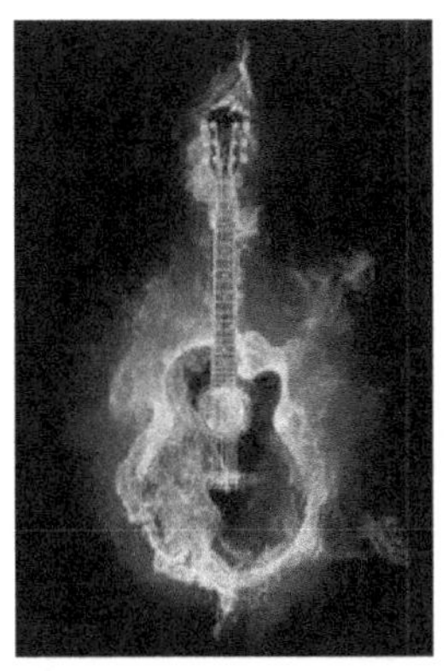

Bono, Lizzy and the Rats

Gabriel Murray

Copyright © 2022

Dun Emer Press